# THE WAY PEOPLE LIVE

# Life in America During the 1960s

Titles in The Way People Live series include:

Cowboys in the Old West
Games of Ancient Rome
Life Among the Great Plains Indians
Life Among the Ibo Women of Nigeria
Life Among the Indian Fighters
Life Among the Pirates
Life Among the Samurai
Life Among the Vikings
Life During the Black Death
Life During the Crusades
Life During the French Revolution
Life During the Gold Rush
Life During the Great Depression
Life During the Middle Ages
Life During the Renaissance
Life During the Russian Revolution
Life During the Spanish Inquisition
Life in a Japanese American Internment
  Camp
Life in a Medieval Castle
Life in a Nazi Concentration Camp
Life in Ancient Athens
Life in Ancient China
Life in Ancient Egypt
Life in Ancient Greece
Life in Ancient Rome
Life in a Medieval Monastery

Life in a Wild West Show
Life in Charles Dickens's England
Life in Communist Russia
Life in Genghis Khan's Mongolia
Life in the Amazon Rain Forest
Life in the American Colonies
Life in the Elizabethan Theater
Life in the Hitler Youth
Life in the North During the Civil War
Life in the South During the Civil War
Life in the Warsaw Ghetto
Life in Tokyo
Life in War-Torn Bosnia
Life of a Medieval Knight
Life of a Nazi Soldier
Life of a Roman Slave
Life of a Roman Soldier
Life of a Slave on a Southern Plantation
Life on Alcatraz
Life on a Medieval Pilgrimage
Life on an African Slave Ship
Life on an Everest Expedition
Life on Ellis Island
Life on the American Frontier
Life on the Oregon Trail
Life on the Underground Railroad
Life Under the Jim Crow Laws

THE WAY PEOPLE LIVE

# Life in America During the 1960s

**by**
**Stuart A. Kallen**

Lucent Books, P.O. Box 289011, San Diego, CA 92198-9011

Library of Congress Cataloging-in-Publication Data

Kallen, Stuart A., 1955–
    Life in America during the 1960s / by Stuart A. Kallen.
        p. cm. — (The way people live)
Includes bibliographical references and index.
    Summary: Discusses life in 1960s America, including prosperity, baby
boomers, African-Americans, Vietnam, protesters, and the changing role of
women.
    ISBN 1-56006-790-X (alk. paper)
    1. United States—History—1961–1969—Juvenile literature. 2. United States—
Social conditions—1960–1980—Juvenile literature. 3. United States—Social
life and customs—1945–1970—Juvenile literature. 4. Nineteen sixties—
Juvenile literature. [1. United States—History—1961–1969. 2. United States—
Social life and customs—1945–1970. 3. Nineteen sixties.] I. Title. II. Series.
    E841 .K27 2001
    973.923—dc21

                                                                    00-011083

# Contents

# Discovering the Humanity in Us All

Books in The Way People Live series focus on groups of people in a wide variety of circumstances, settings, and time periods. Some books focus on different cultural groups, others, on people in a particular historical time period, while others cover people involved in a specific event. Each book emphasizes the daily routines, personal and historical struggles, and achievements of people from all walks of life.

To really understand any culture, it is necessary to strip the mind of the common notions we hold about groups of people. These stereotypes are the archenemies of learning. It does not even matter whether the stereotypes are positive or negative; they are confining and tight. Removing them is a challenge that's not easily met, as anyone who has ever tried it will admit. Ideas that do not fit into the templates we create are unwelcome visitors—ones we would prefer remain quietly in a corner or forgotten room.

The cowboy of the Old West is a good example of such confining roles. The cowboy was courageous, yet soft-spoken. His time (it is always a he, in our template) was spent alternatively saving a rancher's daughter from certain death on a runaway stagecoach, or shooting it out with rustlers. At times, of course, he was likely to get a little crazy in town after a trail drive, but for the most part, he was the epitome of inner strength. It is disconcerting to find out that the cowboy is human, even a bit childish. Can it really be true that cowboys would line up to help the cook on the trail drive grind coffee, just hoping he would give them a little stick of peppermint candy that came with the coffee shipment? The idea of tough cowboys vying with one another to help "Coosie" (as they called their cooks) for a bit of candy seems silly and out of place.

So is the vision of Eskimos playing video games and watching MTV, living in prefab housing in the Arctic. It just does not fit with what "Eskimo" means. We are far more comfortable with snow igloos and whale blubber, harpoons and kayaks.

Although the cultures dealt with in Lucent's The Way People Live series are often historically and socially well known, the emphasis is on the personal aspects of life. Groups of people, while unquestionably affected by their politics and their governmental structures, are more than those institutions. How do people in a particular time and place educate their children? What do they eat? And how do they build their houses? What kinds of work do they do? What kinds of games do they enjoy? The answers to these questions bring these cultures to life. People's lives are revealed in the particulars and only by knowing the particulars can we understand these cultures' will to survive and their moments of weakness and greatness.

This is not to say that understanding politics does not help to understand a culture. There is no question that the Warsaw ghetto, for example, was a culture that was brought about by the politics and social ideas of Adolf

Hitler and the Third Reich. But the Jews who were crowded together in the ghetto cannot be understood by the Reich's politics. Their life was a day-to-day battle for existence, and the creativity and methods they used to prolong their lives is a vital story of human perseverance that would be denied by focusing only on the institutions of Hitler's Germany. Knowing that children as young as five or six outwitted Nazi guards on a daily basis, that Jewish policemen helped the Germans control the ghetto, that children attended secret schools in the ghetto and even earned diplomas—these are the things that reveal the fabric of life, that can inspire, intrigue, and amaze.

Books in The Way People Live series allow both the casual reader and the student to see humans as victims, heroes, and onlookers. And although humans act in ways that can fill us with feelings of sorrow and revulsion, it is important to remember that "hero," "predator," and "victim" are dangerous terms. Heaping undue pity or praise on people reduces them to objects, and strips them of their humanity.

Seeing the Jews of Warsaw only as victims is to deny their humanity. Seeing them only as they appear in surviving photos, staring at the camera with infinite sadness, is limiting, both to them and to those who want to understand them. To an object of pity, the only appropriate response becomes "Those poor creatures!" and that reduces both the quality of their struggle and the depth of their despair. No one is served by such two-dimensional views of people and their cultures.

With this in mind, The Way People Live series strives to flesh out the traditional, two-dimensional views of people in various cultures and historical circumstances. Using a wide variety of primary quotations—the words not only of the politicians and government leaders, but of the real people whose lives are being examined—each book in the series attempts to show an honest and complete picture of a culture removed from our own by time or space.

By examining cultures in this way, the reader will notice not only the glaring differences from his or her own culture, but also will be struck by the similarities. For indeed, people share common needs—warmth, good company, stability, and affirmation from others. Ultimately, seeing how people really live, or have lived, can only enrich our understanding of ourselves.

# A Nation Divided

Although the 1960s are long past, events and influences of that turbulent era continue to color American culture. Looking back, the early sixties seem as flat and gray as the old, grainy black-and-white comedy shows still showing on cable TV. High school fashion for girls included bobbed hair, pleated skirts, and saddle shoes. Clean-cut boys wore crew cuts, button-down sweaters, and penny loafers—some even wore ties to college classes. A Friday night date might have been a movie, a cruise in the family automobile, and a hamburger at a local soda shop eaten while listening to saccharine-sweet crooners such as Frankie Avalon on the jukebox.

## A Culture Transformed

Within a relatively short span of ten years, America became almost unrecognizable from that black-and-white picture. By 1970 the United States experienced a cultural transformation that was truly mind-boggling—even to those who lived through it. Although it is difficult to generalize about the way all people lived during a ten-year period, the sixties were marked by several large groups of people who lived similar lives.

In the mid-sixties, huge numbers of the young—and not so young—began to smoke marijuana. Within those few years, millions of people began to take the psychedelic drug LSD. This was the first time in American history that such a large percentage of people had experimented with illegal drugs. Crew cuts and saddle shoes disappeared under an avalanche of long hair, beads, and kaleidoscopic-colored psychedelic clothing.

At the same time, the United States was engaged in a bloody war in Vietnam that looked more unwinnable with every passing year. In spite of the fact that tens of thousands of American soldiers were being killed—and hundreds of thousands wounded—the government continued to promise victory. This message was lost on many when the nightly news continued to show a steady barrage of pictures of American soldiers dying in the jungles of Vietnam.

About 20 percent of the eighteen- to twenty-five-year-old men called on to fight the war were drafted—involuntarily ordered into military service. The white middle-class men who could afford to go to college, however, were often given deferments and could avoid the draft. It was mostly men who were minorities, poor, or lived in rural areas who were drafted. Millions of others feared that they would be drafted if the war continued.

A huge antiwar movement sprang up among middle-class white students on high school and college campuses. From New York to California, students began to fight authority, often in the form of local police and National Guard troops who were called on to quell disturbances. By the end of the decade, TV screens were often filled with pictures of America's best-educated—and richest—generation battling government troops on street corners. Whenever a new escalation in the war was made by the president, protesters marched as police tear gas filled the air.

The situation was even worse in the inner-city neighborhoods of big cities. Although the Supreme Court had guaranteed equal education and integration for blacks in the 1950s, reforms were slow in coming. African Americans continued to suffer with the worst schools, the poorest-paying jobs, and institutionalized racism from the mostly white police forces that patrolled their neighborhoods.

Black neighborhoods in Los Angeles, Cleveland, New Jersey, and elsewhere were wracked with riots in 1965, 1966, and when Martin Luther King Jr. was assassinated in 1968. The army was often called in to restore order, and the streets were filled with soldiers, tanks, and guns. To some observers, America was beginning to resemble Vietnam. Meanwhile, some black leaders during that period called for the complete

*A demonstrator and a police officer engage in a shouting match at an antiwar demonstration in Madison, Wisconsin.*

overthrow of the U.S. government, as did some white antiwar protesters.

As blacks struggled for their rights and students organized against the war, it became apparent to many that women were often treated as second-class citizens. At the beginning of the sixties, there were some female professionals such as doctors and lawyers. But most women who had jobs were secretaries, food service workers, or domestics. A large percentage of women stayed at home to raise their families while their husbands went to work every day. Even within the various social movements, women were delegated to chores such as making coffee and typing position papers. As the decade came to a close, however, women began raising their voices for equal rights.

These large world-changing events had a profound impact on the lives of average citizens as the drug and sexual experimentation of the counterculture movement was adopted by millions of formerly sober middle-class adults. By the early 1970s, the daily lives of average Americans had been transformed beyond recognition. Jane and Michael Stern describe this phenomenon in *Sixties People:*

> By the end of the sixties, the weirdest thing a person could be was average. At a time when it seemed that everyone was possessed by an unquenchable thirst to be extravagant, exaggerated, way out, hairy, and revolutionary, acting normal started to look like the freakiest lifestyle of all.[1]

## Counterculture to Mainstream Culture

Although there were many difficult changes in people's lives during the sixties, positive influences from that era have become part of the fabric of American culture. While America still has problems with racial inequality, the almost total segregation experienced by blacks in the early sixties has been all but eliminated. Hispanic, Asian, and Native Americans have become an integral part of the culture. And women now take for granted their right to work at any career they choose. Other movements that grew out of the sixties, such as the ecology and the health food movements, have become ingrained in American society.

However, some of the divisions apparent in society in the 1960s remain in place today. The culture clash between those on the political right and those on the left remains, often intensifying over issues that originated in the sixties, such as abortion, gay rights, and the war on drugs. In spite of the political differences, however, in the 1990s everyone from President Bill Clinton to conservative Speaker of the House Newt Gingrich admitted to smoking marijuana, as did several of the candidates for president in 2000—something that would have been unheard of in the sixties.

Understandably, many people in the twenty-first century have become tired of hearing about the 1960s. And as the baby boom generation grows older and dies, a large percentage of Americans alive today were not even born in the sixties. But sixties culture is everywhere—one can scarcely turn on the TV, radio, or even sign onto the Internet without seeing or hearing something influenced or created in the sixties. The counterculture of decades past has become the dominant culture today. So while the hippie flower power of the Summer of Love is long gone, the love of peace, equal rights, and ecology has become ingrained in American society as the counterculture has become the prevailing culture.

# Mainstream America

For a large percentage of Americans, the early 1960s were similar to the 1950s. It was a time of home and family, with fathers going to work every morning to support their families while mothers stayed at home to raise the children. The average white family owned a home in the suburbs, bought a new car every few years, and was able to enjoy a comfortable lifestyle that was not available to the average citizen before World War II.

## Family Life

The relatively new American prosperity meant that people could afford to have children at a younger age. In the early sixties, women married in larger numbers than ever before. In 1940 only 42 percent of women were married by the age of twenty-four, but by 1960 that number had jumped to 70 percent. And in the 1960s, the average age for marriage was lower than ever before—or since. The average age for men to marry in the 1960s was twenty-two, for women, nineteen. There was great social pressure to marry, and young people were widely encouraged to wed by scholars and the media. According to Myron A. Marty in *Daily Life in the United States: 1960–1990,*

> Popular magazines extolled the virtues of marriage and family life, and movies and television programs portrayed them as romantic ideals. Psychologists, educators, journalists, and religious leaders rein-

forced the idea that marriage was necessary for personal well-being. Failure to marry suggested some sort of personal deficiency.[2]

With marriage came children. Although the birth control pill was introduced in 1960, it was not widely used until the mid-sixties. In fact, in 1960, 4.25 million babies—a record number—were born in the United States, compared to about half that many in 1940. And American families were remarkably stable at the beginning of the decade. Many states enforced strict antidivorce laws, making it difficult for most couples to separate. In the early sixties, the divorce rate was only about 10 percent, compared with over 50 percent in the 1990s.

## A Home in the Suburbs

Families needed homes to live in, and the sixties were a time when thousands of housing developments were springing up all over the country. In the early sixties, a large percentage of American men over forty were veterans of World War II, which was fought between 1941–45. After the war, the government provided veterans with low-interest mortgages and subsidized college educations. In the 1950s, backed by the G.I. Bill, millions of families moved into inexpensive assembly-line housing built in new suburbs on the edges of big cities. By the 1960s, these families were well settled into their suburban neighborhoods.

*Many veterans of World War II moved to suburban neighborhoods with their families after receiving low-interest mortgages to buy homes.*

Families could buy three-bedroom houses with modern appliances, garages, and lawns for as little as $15,000. An unprecedented number of people took advantage of the low-cost housing market, and by 1960, for the first time, there were more Americans living in suburbs than in cities. A large percentage of these new suburbanites were white people of European descent whose relatives had come to the United States in the nineteenth and early twentieth centuries. There were few nonwhite people from foreign lands in the sixties suburbs because the United States had enacted strict laws limiting immigration in the 1920s, and these restrictions were still in place during the 1960s.

The suburbs did bring some changes, however. The new housing developments became a melting pot of sorts for the children of the European immigrants who had remained separated from other nationalities when they had previously lived in big cities. According to David Farber in *The Great Age of Dreams: America in the 1960s,*

[The people in the new housing tracts had] grown up in relatively parochial and exclusive ethnic communities [and were now recasting] themselves . . . in the [new] communities of suburbia as just plain middle-class white Americans. . . . Catholics, and with greater restrictions, Jews mixed with Protestants in these new communities.[3]

When these people moved next door to one another, they began to distance themselves from their European heritage, and ethnic and religious differences were cast aside in favor of patriotism and conformity. Most families strove to be the same as the people who lived next door. They dressed alike, drove similar cars, and watched the same television shows.

The inhabitants of these new suburbs had lived through poverty during the Great Depression and fought in Europe and Asia in World War II. When they were growing up, only wealthy people had washers and dryers, drove new cars, and owned their own homes. Although their suburban lifestyles were often described in disparaging terms by social critics, many suburbanites considered themselves supremely lucky after the hardships they had suffered.

Having fought for their country, the middle-class people in the suburbs rarely questioned government policy. Social critics Michael and Jane Stern describe the typical early sixties family living in the suburbs:

The way Mr. and Mrs. Average saw things, they [were] citizens of a patriotic race whose men proudly wore enameled flag pins on the lapels of their suit jackets. They lived in an orderly land of shined shoes, pressed handkerchiefs, and weekly trips to the barbershop for a trim and a chat. Children sat at school desks with folded hands and called their elders "ma'am" and "sir." On Sunday everybody went to church, ate Mom's chicken dinner, then settled into their wood-paneled dens, where they were entertained by acrobats, jugglers, and [puppets] on "The Ed Sullivan Show." They lived in a happy community of happy people just like themselves: hardworking, meat-

eating, Chevrolet-driving, God-fearing, flag-waving, law-abiding, polite-speaking taxpayers who all shared the same idea of what was right and good. It was swell. . . .[4]

## A Time of Abundance

The hardworking suburbanites were living in a time of unparalleled affluence. The post–World War II economic boom in the United States was the largest in American history at that time. Average individual incomes were growing at 6 percent a year, and overall family incomes had doubled since the end of the war. And this American prosperity included a broad segment of the public. Although 20 percent lived at or below the poverty rate, the annual gross national product (the total market value of all the goods and services produced) had soared 250 percent in the same period. As historian Farber writes: "What those numbers meant for a majority of

| Facts About America During the 1960s | |
|---|---|
| Population | 177,830,000 |
| Unemployment | 3,852,000 |
| National Debt | $286.3 billion |
| Average Yearly Salary | $4,743 |
| Minimum Wage | $1.00 per hour |
| Life Expectancy | |
| Males | 66.6 years |
| Females | 73.1 years |

Americans was a material life, in world-historical terms, of incredible abundance. In 1960, America was the richest nation the world had ever seen."[5]

In this time of abundance, it was usually only the man in the family who worked. Even with one wage earner, the average family was able to afford a new car every few years, a college education for every child, and a wide range of newly introduced consumer products such as color TVs, electric coffee makers, toothbrushes, typewriters, and can openers.

During this era, it was not necessary to possess a college education to partake in the American dream. Even blue-collar workers were able to afford material goods only dreamed of by their parents. Farber writes about the workers who built cars such as Chevrolets, Pontiacs, Buicks, and Cadillacs for General Motors:

GM's unionized assembly-line workers—many without high school diplomas—drove new cars, bought [second homes such as] cottages by the lake, and looked forward to guaranteed raises and generous pensions. High wages meant that very few [unionized autoworkers'] wives worked (nor could they . . . given the sexism male employers and employees took for granted). The United Auto Workers [Union], protected by laws passed during the [Depression], had demanded and received a smorgasbord of wages and benefits; complacent management, rather than face strikes at a time of high demand for their products, went along. As auto executive Lee Iacocca recalled: "In those days we could afford to be generous. Because we had a lock on the market, we could continually spend more money on labor and simply pass the additional costs

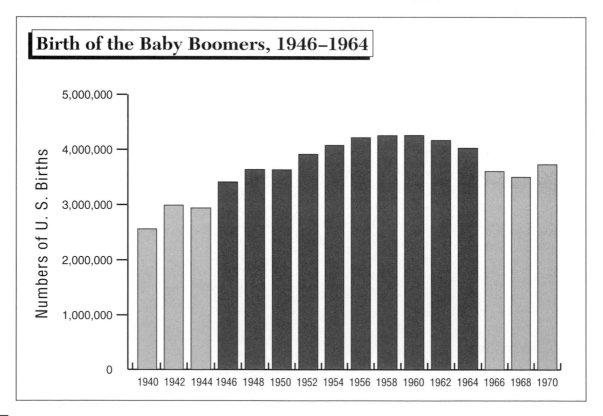

**Birth of the Baby Boomers, 1946–1964**

along to the consumer in the form of price increases."[6]

## The Baby Boomers

Prosperous workers like the autoworkers could afford families, and during the postwar era, the United States experienced a "baby boom," which formed a huge demographic "bubble" that profoundly influenced American culture with its ever-changing tastes in music, food, and fashion.

Between 1946 and 1964, over 76 million children were born in the United States—more than 4 million a year after the mid-1950s. Even with very little foreign immigration, this caused the population of the United States to swell from almost 140 million in 1940, to 180.6 million in 1960, and 205 million by 1970. Marty explains the consequences of this baby boom:

> Neighborhoods teemed with children during out-of-school hours. To the playtime repertory of earlier years—swing sets, sandboxes, tricycles, bicycles, balls, and bats—parents added Frisbees, hula hoops, and Barbie dolls, plastic playthings introduced in 1957, 1958, and 1959. For many, playtime gave way to Brownies and Cub-pack meetings, Girl Scout or Boy Scout or 4-H activities, Little League (for boys), and after-school religious instruction and church choir practice. That meant lots of driving for mothers; in families with only one car, negotiating carpools and juggling schedules became an art.[7]

Children born during the postwar baby boom began to reach their teenage years during the sixties. In 1964 seventeen-year-olds comprised the largest age group in the country, and there were 24 million people between the ages of fifteen and twenty-four. By 1970 that number had grown to 35 million. By 1966 almost 50 percent of the people in America were under the age of twenty-six.

These young people were the first generation raised on television, TV dinners, and rock and roll. Most white teens attended newly constructed schools in the suburbs and, with after-school jobs, often had weekly incomes of about $20—higher than the average disposable income of a family of four in the 1940s.

The baby boom generation was also extremely well educated. At the beginning of the Depression in 1929, most young people were working full-time by the time they were eighteen, with only 20 percent of American teens graduating from high school. In the 1960s, over 75 percent were high school graduates. At the beginning of World War II, only 16 percent of American students went to college after high school. In 1965 that figure was about 50 percent. This meant, according to Farber, "a much greater percentage of young people stayed together in the same youth-centered institutional system and were taught many of the same things for far longer than any previous generation."[8]

In short, the baby boom generation had a better education, more money and possessions, and brighter hopes for the future than any other generation that preceded them. And the influence of this demographic group was felt throughout society. According to John Javin and Gordon Javan in 60s!: "Youth was in and everybody wanted to look young, feel young, act young. Young people dictated style and fashion."[9]

## A Changing Diet

Teens not only dictated styles and fashion, but also the types of food consumed by American families. Potato chips, pretzels, and other snack

# President Kennedy

When forty-three-year-old John F. Kennedy was sworn in as the thirty-fifth president of the United States in January 1961, he was the youngest man to ever hold that office. He was replacing seventy-year-old Dwight D. Eisenhower, and the symbolism of this change in power was potent. Kennedy said in his inaugural address that the "torch has been passed to a new generation of Americans," and his words proved prophetic. In *Good Times: An Oral History of America in the Nineteen Sixties*, school administrator Don Ferguson describes the Kennedy charisma:

"Kennedy came along with a new, fresh, young image. . . . Everything [the Kennedys] did showed that America was alive and active. Family ski trips. Football games at [their home in] Hyannis Port, [Massachusetts,] riding around in the golf cart, going out in the ocean on a boat, going to nightclubs. [The president's wife] Jackie with her new hair styles—everybody started getting the Jackie hairdos. . . . To run a country it takes more than just mechanics. It takes a psychology. It takes a confidence, and you don't build that confidence by a bunch of old men or women who plod around and don't do anything very stimulating and exciting, or who don't take much advantage of the things that are good about this country. They were enjoying entertainment, having music in the parlors, and giving out awards. The Space Age was hatched. There was a whole batch of things to bring a whole new feeling of enthusiasm."

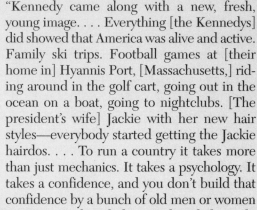

*Many believe that the Kennedy presidency brought new enthusiasm to America.*

foods were available in the 1950s. By the sixties, however, the food industry in America had begun to produce a wide variety of so-called "junk food" using processes and chemicals never before used for making food.

Baby boomer children munched on brightly colored, sugary breakfast cereal in the morning, "pressed meat" cold cuts on fluffy white bread for lunch, and canned ravioli or frozen TV dinners at night. The food was laden with large doses of sugar, fat, and salt, along with unpronounceable chemical additives and preservatives. All told, the food industry in the 1960s was using over three thousand barely tested additives in food.

As the move toward convenience foods increased, more Americans began eating outside of the home. With the growth of the fast-food industry, hamburgers, french fries, and milk shakes began to take up a larger portion of the American diet. By 1960 McDonald's founder Ray Kroc had opened about a hundred of his famous hamburger stands throughout the country. By 1967 the hamburger franchise, ten years old, had a thousand restaurants and claimed to have sold over a billion burgers. Nationally, a new McDonald's was opening at the rate of one per day, and by the early seventies, McDonald's had surpassed the U.S. Army as the largest daily supplier of food in America.

With the success of McDonald's, a wave of hamburger, roast beef, pizza, and chicken franchises were constructed at nearly every busy intersection. As the decade progressed, many "mom-and-pop" restaurants were replaced by McDonald's, Arby's, Burger King, Kentucky Fried Chicken, and others. In less than ten years, American eating habits had been transformed by a huge $250 billion–a-year fast-food industry.

## Television

The move toward fast food was enhanced by television. Not only did commercials advertise the food, but people began to leave their dining rooms to eat in front of their televisions.

In 1950 only 4.4 million Americans owned television sets. By 1960 that number had grown to 50 million, meaning 90 percent of all American households owned at least one television. The most popular shows in the early sixties featured tough-talking cowboys engaged in gunfights with villains in black hats. Between 1960 and 1962 the top four TV shows were *Gunsmoke, Wagon Train, Have Gun—Will Travel,* and *Bonanza. Bonanza,* a show about a father and three sons in the Cartwright family, was the most watched TV show between 1964 and 1967. Javin and Javan explain how this show symbolized America's shared values:

> [The Cartwrights] played fair and they worked hard. They were humble, they went to church, and yet, they had a sense of humor. . . . They were kind to strangers. They stood up for the underdog, they cared about people. And they were . . . rich. . . . "Bonanza" was so popular that people often refused to believe that [their ranch called] the Ponderosa was fictional.[10]

By the mid-sixties, however, cowboy shows gave way to situation comedies, many of which poked gentle fun at the American dream. One of the most popular shows of the 1960s was *The Beverly Hillbillies,* which was about the Clampetts, a family of poor Arkansas "mountaineers" who became rich when they discovered oil on their farm. The Clampetts moved to America's richest neighborhood, Beverly Hills, in Los Angeles, California. Although critics panned the

*During the early sixties, cowboy shows were the most popular TV entertainment.*

From 1960 to 1966, *The Flintstones* was an enormously popular cartoon show, and the first to run in "prime time"—the hours between 7 and 10 P.M. In *Sixties People*, Jane and Michael Stern write that the show was so well loved because Americans saw themselves reflected in this "modern Stone Age family."

"'The Flintstones' was . . . about [an average] suburban family . . . except for the twist that they live in the Stone Age. [The characters] ride in stone cars, speak on stone telephones, play 'rock' music on a turntable that uses a prehistoric bird's beak for a needle, and . . . have all the modern [features] of suburbia,

including bowling night, home swimming pools, baby sitting, dogs, etc. [Father] Fred is a construction worker; the motto of the company where he works is 'Own Your Own Cave and Be Secure. . . .'

Based on the popularity of 'The Flintstones,' [the producers] launched 'The Jetsons' in 1962. The Jetsons are just like the Flintstones, except they live in the twenty-first century. . . . [and] lived out their commonplace days amidst rocket ships, boomerang-shaped coffee tables, and self-propelled vacuum cleaners.

The 'gimmick' of both 'The Flintstones' and 'The Jetsons' is that both families are absolutely average! Each of the characters is a dull, predictable cliché; the joy of the shows is seeing Fred and Wilma Flintstone or George and Jane Jetson make a bizarre world into a completely familiar, middle-class one. Thus, the Averages could bask in the monotony of their own lives playing out in centuries past and future, the implication being that civilization as they knew it, in all its comfortable mediocrity, would never end."

*According to some critics, the TV show "The Jetsons" depicted a typical, middle-class life in America.*

show, average Americans loved it, keeping it in the top-twenty most popular shows from 1962 to 1969.

During this era, California had become the most populated state in the country, and mil-

lions of people were moving there every year. And, as Farber writes,

like the Clampetts, people from diverse backgrounds had uprooted themselves, left their kinfolk and community behind them, and started life anew in California. . . . Just as important, the Clampetts' sudden wealth served as a fun-house mirror for the relatively new prosperity millions of Americans enjoyed by the early 1960s. While few viewers could expect a Beverly Hills mansion, many who had lived through the Great Depression in urban tenements or broken-down farmhouses did find themselves living in all-electric California-style ranch houses and were aware of the distance they had traveled.[11]

Sixties television, however, had a dark show that revealed some of the negative aspects of American society. *The Twilight Zone*, which aired on Friday nights from 1959 to 1962, dealt with serious issues such as racism, mob violence, materialism, and the dangers of rigid conformity. Although the show had a cult following, it did not last long in the optimistic sixties. Most Americans preferred tough cowboys, prehistoric cartoon families, and bumbling hillbillies to the weighty lessons of *The Twilight Zone*.

## A Promise Shattered

Perhaps the main television event of the 1960s occurred when the optimism and promise of the early sixties were shattered on November 22, 1963, when President John F. Kennedy was assassinated in Dallas, Texas. Over 175 million

*Americans were shocked and horrified when President John F. Kennedy was assassinated in 1963.*

people—93 percent of all Americans—watched the events that followed on television. All three major networks suspended regular programming—and all commercials—to broadcast the breaking news. Two days later, Lee Harvey Oswald, Kennedy's alleged assassin, was shot on live television as police were transferring him from the Dallas County Jail.

Almost everyone in America saw Oswald being shot in the stomach—a first in television history. With these two bizarre consecutive murders, America's postwar innocence seemed to be instantly destroyed. As sixties antiwar leader Tom Hayden later wrote: "We followed the breaking news, watched the murder of Oswald over and over [on television], and let the event etch its way like a toxic acid into our consciousness. This was the most unexpected happening of my life, having been raised in the climate of a stable American presidency . . . in an unstable and warring world."[12]

On Sunday, November 24, with the Thanksgiving holiday only days away, almost everyone in America watched Kennedy's funeral on television. After America's youngest president was laid to rest, regular TV programming resumed. A following study by Social Research Inc. stated that the decision to return to regular broadcasting after more than two hundred hours of commercial-free coverage of Kennedy's death, "set an orderly limit on the period of mourning and told the public, now we should all get back to the task of living."[13]

The new president, Lyndon Johnson, appointed a blue-ribbon panel, headed by Earl Warren, the chief justice of the Supreme Court, to investigate Kennedy's murder. The 469-page Warren Report later stated that Oswald acted alone. Americans were not convinced, and soon dozens of books appeared that attempted to trace the president's murder to everyone from the Central Intelligence Agency (CIA) to the Mafia to Cuban dictator Fidel Castro. A serious, lingering doubt had been planted in the public's mind, and in 1965 a poll showed that over 50 percent of Americans believed that there was a high-level conspiracy behind Kennedy's assassination and that his murderers were never punished. Hayden explains the affect this uncertainty had on his generation:

> [If Oswald did not act] alone . . . then we were dealing with a violent conspiracy perhaps reaching into the [highest levels of the] power elite itself. [That] notion was enough to unsettle my world. The scent of evil and the cloud of tragedy, forces beyond knowing or control, were now present in my life in a more personal way than ever before. I cried for John Kennedy's . . . family, for myself.

> The tragic consciousness of the sixties generation began here, and would continue and grow. Deepening that consciousness in the [following] weeks was my sense that the truth of the assassination was being covered up, that it might never be disclosed or agreed upon, and that we would be left to make whatever image of this national [murder] our own fantasies or fears, hopes or illusions required. To conclude, as I did, that a conspiracy of more than Oswald was involved, meant living with the certainty that John Kennedy's killers were still among us.[14]

## The Intrusion of Vietnam

After Kennedy's death, President Lyndon B. Johnson, or LBJ, quickly escalated a war in the little-known Asian country of Vietnam. Although he could not know it at the time, the government's "mission" in Vietnam would soon shake the United States to its very foundations, affecting the lives of average Americans in profound ways. By 1962 the United States had already sent eleven thousand advisers to help the South Vietnamese fight the communist forces of North Vietnam. These operations were largely secret and made few headlines. In August 1964, however, the U.S. Congress gave LBJ unlimited powers to wage a war in Vietnam—without actually declaring war.

On March 8, 1965, fifty thousand U.S. Marine combat ground forces landed in Da Nang, South Vietnam, ostensibly to protect the U.S. Air Force base there. By the end of the year, another 150,000 marines and army troops would be stationed in Da Nang.

Almost as soon as Johnson ordered the first wave of marines to Vietnam, protests erupted on college campuses across the country. Coincidentally, about 2 million baby boomers were first reaching draft age in 1964, and suddenly this group of teenagers who had been raised in peace and prosperity faced the very real danger of having to fight a foreign enemy in the jungles of Vietnam.

Average Americans quickly divided between two camps, those who supported the war, called Hawks, and those who opposed the war, called Doves. While some opposed the war on moral grounds, many of those against the war were teenagers who might be drafted. And most who supported the war were their fathers who had fought in World War II. Suddenly, many average American families were ripped in two as fierce arguments broke out over the morality of the rapidly escalating war, as Farber explains:

> Most older and working-class Americans who did not support the war did not dislike it enough to take action or did not consider it appropriate to publicly protest their government's policy. Most believed that politics meant voting and, perhaps, bringing their individual concerns to the attention of an

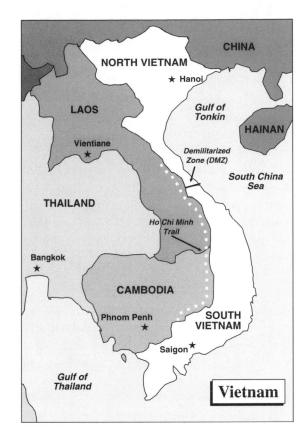

elected official. Social order and civility, most Americans believed, depended on people not pushing their political views into anyone else's face. And maintaining order and proper behavior meant more to many older, non-college-educated Americans than did their discomfort with the war.[15]

While the majority did not want to protest the war, they most certainly would have noticed the economic liability of the conflict. In 1966 alone, the government spent $12 billion on the Vietnam War that was not included in the federal budget. Taxes were raised, and combined with other economic problems, the inflation rate began to noticeably rise. For average citizens, this meant that the price of food, clothing, cars, shelter, and other basic necessities became more expensive with each passing year.

# A Polarized Nation

By 1967 America had become a polarized nation with some people supporting the Vietnam War and others adamantly opposing it. In addition to the war, the widespread use of the psychedelic drug LSD was also causing havoc in middle-class society.

In the 1950s, the CIA had begun experimenting with the drug LSD to see if it could be used for brainwashing and mind-control purposes. When these tests failed because the drug was too unpredictable, the government began paying college students to take LSD in order to record their physiological reactions. By 1965 some of the students who had participated in these experiments began stealing the drug from college laboratories and openly distributing it in hippie neighborhoods. The result was the most widespread, unregulated drug experiment in history.

People who took LSD often experienced drastic changes in their personalities, sometimes losing their inhibitions, quitting their jobs, or dropping out of school. And millions of average American households were affected when teenagers began to experiment with drugs. Even many of those young people who did not take drugs began to emulate the lifestyles of the counterculture, growing long hair and ignoring or mocking traditional social and religious values.

Of course not everybody was taking drugs and dropping out of society, but hippies and antiwar protesters received a great deal of attention in the sixties media. Even though much of that attention was negative, millions of families with teenagers began to suffer the effects of what came to be known as the "generation gap." Arguments with parents over politics, the war, psychedelic rock music, drugs, long hair, and outrageous clothes caused thousands of teenagers to leave their secure suburban roots behind, preferring life in rapidly expanding hippie neighborhoods.

Few parents—raised to obey orders in the war, work hard, and strictly conform with their neighbors—understood this brave new world. The days of crew cuts, unquestioned patriotism, and polite schoolchildren of earlier years suddenly seemed to be a forgotten part of a long-distant past.

# African Americans in the Sixties

While the 1960s were prosperous years for a majority of Americans, about 20 percent of the people in the United States lived below the poverty line. Some of the poor were white people who lived in rural areas. A large majority, however, were African Americans who had been left out of the American dream through neglect and racism.

In the early sixties, black Americans faced prejudice and discrimination in almost every aspect of life, from jobs and housing to education. In the South, where 60 percent of all African Americans lived, blacks were deprived of equal voting rights until 1964. They were even denied the right to sit at the same lunch counter or use the same public rest room as white people.

## Discrimination in Jobs and Housing

In spite of their poor treatment at home, millions of African American men bravely served overseas in World War II. After bringing

*During the 1960s segregated facilities were common, especially in the South.*

# LBJ's Great Society

The poverty experienced by 20 percent of Americans in the 1960s did not go unnoticed by people in the federal government. In 1964 President Lyndon Johnson declared a "War on Poverty" and proposed a wide range of federal programs. Optimistically referred to as the "Great Society" programs, Johnson proposed to improve public transportation, distribute food stamps, supply medical care, and improve education for America's poor. Johnson introduced the Great Society programs at a commencement address at the University of Michigan in Ann Arbor on May 22, 1964. Quoted by Peter B. Levy in *America in the Sixties Right, Left, and Center*, the president told the crowd:

"Your imagination, your initiative, and your indignation will determine whether we build a society where progress is the servant of our needs, or a society where old values and new visions are buried under unbridled growth. For in your time we have the opportunity to move not only toward the rich society and the powerful society, but upward to the Great Society. The Great Society rests on abundance and liberty for all. It demands an end to poverty and racial injustice, to which we are totally committed in our time. But that is just the beginning. The Great Society is a place where every child can find knowledge to enrich his mind and to enlarge his talents. It is a place where leisure is a welcome chance to build and reflect, not a feared cause of boredom and restlessness. It is a place where the city of man serves not only the needs of the body and the demands of commerce, but the desire for beauty and the hunger for community."

democracy to Western Europe and Japan, however, the veterans returned to the United States, where they were denied the most basic rights guaranteed by the U.S. Constitution.

Before the war, most poor Americans lived in rural areas, where they were farmhands and sharecroppers. The postwar invention of mechanized farming equipment forced an estimated 2.3 million mostly black farmworkers to move to cities, and by 1960 over half of America's poor lived in large cities or medium-sized towns. Although a majority of African Americans lived in the South, many had migrated north during the war to work at high-paying factory jobs in cities like Detroit, Cleveland, Pittsburgh, and elsewhere. Others moved to Los Angeles, where the defense industry was expanding at a rapid rate. For example, between 1940 and 1945, the black population of the Los Angeles Watts neighborhood doubled.

After the war, however, African Americans were laid off as newly returned white veterans took their places on the assembly lines that were now producing cars, stoves, refrigerators, and other consumer products. Black inner-city neighborhoods, which had been relatively prosperous during the war, were drained of money as black unemployment figures skyrocketed. At the same time, the white exodus to the suburbs in the 1950s left big cities bereft of tax dollars. Stores in black neighborhoods were boarded up, parks fell to ruin, and schools sank to substandard conditions.

Blacks who could afford to leave inner-city neighborhoods faced open discrimination when they tried to move into the new suburbs. Farber writes about the Long Island suburb of Levittown outside of New York City:

In 1960, 82,000 people lived in Long Island's Levittown, the most celebrated of the new suburban subdevelopments, and not one of them was African American. Black families were told by the developers openly not to bother trying to buy a home—they were not welcome. Racial segregation, in the North and West, as well as in the South, was a well accepted fact of life in the new suburbs.[16]

Discrimination was even worse for the first several black families who tried to move into the white suburbs of Chicago—they had their homes burned to the ground by angry neighbors.

In neighborhoods where blacks did live, they generally paid higher rents and faced crowded conditions, because even those who could afford to leave had nowhere else to live. Because demand for rental properties was so high, many landlords did not feel the need to maintain their properties. And banks refused to give mortgages even to qualified people in poor black neighborhoods because of racist lending practices.

These problems were aggravated by the poor job market that existed for blacks. Farber lists the bleak job prospects for African Americans in 1960:

[In] the South no African Americans held political office, no blacks worked as lawyers, doctors, engineers, or executives in white-owned businesses or firms. [In February 1960] the *Atlanta Constitution*, in its race- and gender-segregated want ads, offered black men exactly three jobs: car washer, custodian, and broiler cook. African American women saw six listings for maids, and openings for a salad [preparation] girl, a laundress, and a babysitter.[17]

As a result of such discrimination, not only was black unemployment during the sixties three times higher than that of whites, but up to 50 percent of black adults were unemployed in some areas. The general feeling of hopelessness caused by these conditions created widespread anger in black neighborhoods across the country.

## Integrating Classrooms and Lunch Counters

Although African Americans continued to face discrimination in daily life, the 1950s had been a time of legal gains for blacks. In 1954 the Supreme Court ordered an end to school segregation and instructed schools to immediately allow black enrollment. This courtroom victory, however, did not help integrate schools. In 1960, 99 percent of southern black children continued to attend segregated schools and no African American high school graduates were allowed to attend white colleges in the South.

In the North and West, as well as the South, schools attended by African Americans were overcrowded and underfunded. Dismal conditions and little hope for financial advancement led to high dropout rates. In cities such as Cleveland and Los Angeles, up to 70 percent of inner-city African Americans did not graduate high school.

In spite of the discrimination, by 1960 there were over 200,000 African American college students attending all-black schools in the South. Many African American students belonged to equal rights organizations such as Congress of Racial Equality (CORE) and Southern Christian Leadership Council (SCLC), led by Dr. Martin Luther King Jr., and they were organized and ready to initiate a new decade of protest.

On February 1, 1960, four neatly dressed black male college students entered the Woolworth's department store in Greensboro, North Carolina. The store had a lunch counter that catered to whites only, but the students sat down and ordered coffee. The waitress refused to serve them, and the students sat quietly at the counter until the store closed an hour later. The next day, twenty black students sat at the lunch counter. On the third day, sixty students were refused service.

The idea of using nonviolent sit-ins to integrate lunch counters spread to cities across the South. The students remained on their best behavior, in spite of verbal and physical taunts by white bystanders. John Lewis, who later became a U.S. Congressman, recalls organizing a sit-in:

We made a list of what we called the "Rules of the Sit-in"—the do's and don't's—and we mimeographed it on an old machine and

*Three men participate in a sit-in at a Woolworth's lunch counter in 1960.*

passed it out to all the students. . . . I remember it said things like, "Sit up straight. Don't talk back. Don't laugh. Don't strike back." And at the end it said, "Remember the [nonviolent] teachings of Jesus, Gandhi . . . and Martin Luther King, Jr."[18]

Despite the students' good behavior, police allowed white thugs to assault the protesters, as Lewis recalls:

[A] group of young white men came in and began pulling people off the lunch-counter stools, putting lighted cigarettes out in our hair or faces or down our backs, pouring catsup and hot sauce all over us, pushing us to the floor and beating us. . . . They didn't arrest a single person that beat us, but they arrested all of us and charged us with disorderly conduct.[19]

The next day, five thousand protesters marched on Nashville city hall. Widespread public pressure and negative publicity forced the government into action, and within weeks Tennessee's lunch counters were integrated. Protesters found similar success at restaurants throughout the South.

## Gaining Civil Rights

Throughout the early sixties, African Americans—often joined by white college students from northern cities—continued to fight discrimination in the South. In addition to integrating public facilities, blacks registered large numbers of people to vote.

They continued to face violent retaliation for their actions, however. Several protest organizers had their homes bombed. In addition, thousands of protesters were arrested and beaten by police and angry mobs—dozens were

*Over 250,000 African Americans participate in a civil rights march on Washington, D.C. in 1963.*

killed. Southern whites used rocks, cans, pipes, chains, and guns against protesters while police used tear gas, high-pressure fire hoses, and billy clubs. Those who were arrested were often held weeks without bail.

In the midst of this anger and violence, the March on Washington, sponsored by several black organizations, was held on August 28, 1963. On that hot August afternoon, Dr. Martin Luther King Jr. gave his now-famous "I Have a Dream" speech to 250,000 African Americans who had assembled in front of the Lincoln Memorial. The CBS television network preempted regular programming to carry the day's events, and NBC and ABC televised King's speech only. When the nation saw hundreds of thousands of black citizens peacefully assembled and heard King's eloquent speech, public opinion was galvanized in favor of equal rights and millions of Americans focused for the first time on the plight of blacks in the United States.

The march was attended by well-known black actor Harry Belafonte and other famous people. But, according to the deputy director of the march, Bayard Rustin, quoted in *Voices of Freedom*, the rich and powerful were not on the world stage that day:

> It wasn't the Harry Belafontes and the greats from Hollywood that made the march. What made the march was that black people voted that day with their feet. They came from every state, they came in jalopies, on trains, buses, anything they could get— some walked. There were about three hundred congressmen there, but none of them said a word. We had told them to come, but we wanted to talk with them, they were not to talk to us. And after they came and saw that it was very orderly, that there was fantastic determination, that there were all kinds of people there other than black people, they knew there was a consensus in this country for the [Civil Rights Act]. . . .[20]

With public opinion galvanized in favor of African American equality, Lyndon Johnson was able to pass the Civil Rights Act in 1964, which prohibited discrimination in employment, pubic accommodations, and publicly owned facilities. In 1965 Congress passed the Voting Rights Act, mandating the right to vote for all blacks in every city, town, and county in the United States.

## "Nonviolence Was Outvoted"

As African Americans had seen before with Supreme Court decisions in their favor, the Civil Rights Act and Voting Rights Act did little to change their daily lives. Those laws were aimed mainly at rural southern blacks and did little to address the problems of the African American majority who lived in big cities, where the federal government had less control. And while the nonviolent methods of protest advocated by Dr. King played well to television cameras and white audiences, a large segment of inner-city blacks were angry and frustrated at the lack of progress in their lives. According to black playwright, actor, and musician Stanley Crouch, many blacks, like whites, were greatly influenced by prime-time television programs. Crouch writes in *The Sixties* that black anger was influenced by

> the concepts of manhood, self-defense and "justifiable revenge" that dominated much more television time than did the real suffering of civil rights workers. Every tactic of [Martin Luther King Jr.'s nonviolent protest] was contradicted by weekly war films, swashbucklers [pirates], Westerns, and detective shows. *Men* did not allow women and children to be beaten, hosed, [shocked with cattle prods], or blown up [when bombs were thrown inside their] Sunday schools. Nonviolence both as a tactic and philosophy was outvoted.[21]

Although the problems of inner-city blacks came from a wide variety of causes, it was the police force that was most visible in their daily lives. Most 1960s big-city police departments were overwhelmingly white and male. To those living in black neighborhoods, the police resembled an occupying army that was quick to beat or shoot anyone regardless of their guilt or innocence.

The first major riot of the sixties occurred in the Watts area of Los Angeles, where a neighborhood that was 98 percent black was patrolled by two hundred white police officers.

On August 11, 1965, only five days after President Johnson signed the Voting Rights Act, a typical confrontation with police turned into a bloody uprising.

White police officers pulled over a young black man for a traffic offense, and the driver was drunk and abusive. When police violently restrained the young man, a large crowd gathered and began to throw rocks and bottles. As more police arrived to restore order, the violence exploded through 150 square blocks of the Watts neighborhood. For six days people looted and burned, and by the time the revolt was quelled, more than 34 people had been killed, 865 injured, and 4,000 arrested. Entire blocks were burned to the ground, and property damage was estimated at $45 million. A new chant "Burn, baby, burn" was born as hundreds watched white-owned businesses go up in flames.

## "Nothing but Burnt-up Buildings"

In light of recent gains made by blacks, average Americans—and even many in the Watts neighborhood—were appalled at the violence.

*National Guard officers patrol the Watts neighborhood of Los Angeles after riots erupt in 1965.*

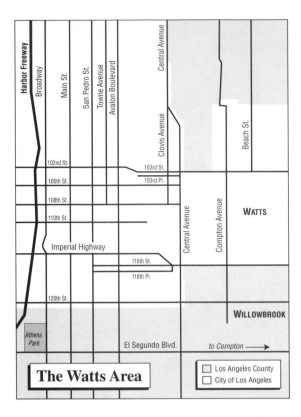

**The Watts Area**

Los Angeles County
City of Los Angeles

The Watts Riots were the first in a long series of black uprisings in the sixties. In 1965 forty-three inner-city neighborhoods were rocked with riots. In 1967 almost every city with a black population experienced a riot, with 167 inner-city neighborhoods going up in flames. In 1968, after Martin Luther King Jr. was assassinated in Memphis, another wave of riots swept the country. During each disturbance, dozens of people were killed by police, National Guard troops, and rioters. Some cities experienced two or even three civil disturbances. In all, over four hundred major and minor riots were recorded in the United States between 1964 and 1969.

A large majority of African Americans living in these neighborhoods were law-abiding citizens who were disgusted by the violence. In fact, the uprisings only contributed to their misery. An unnamed women in Detroit said, "I don't see where the riot accomplished nothing myself but a lot of burnt-up buildings. . . . People couldn't buy a loaf of bread or a quart of milk nowhere in the neighborhood after those riots."[23]

After the fires were put out and order restored, many neighborhoods never recovered. For up to thirty years after the riots, some areas of Watts, Cleveland, Detroit, and elsewhere contained dozens of city blocks full of litter and rubble where stores and houses had once stood.

But government decrees could not quell the anger felt by many inner-city residents. An unnamed rioter explains his cathartic feelings in *The Great Age of Dreams:*

> I felt invincible. . . . Honestly, that is how powerful I felt. I'm not too proud of what I did, looking back. But I held nothing back. I let out all my frustrations with every brick, every bottle that I threw. Many people ran around looting the stores. . . . My only thought about the stores was something like "Those store owners will be furious, but who cares. They aren't black. They don't know what furious really is." Then I picked up a bottle and tried to destroy a TV in the window display. I remembered feeling completely relieved. I unleashed all the emotions that had built up inside, ones I didn't know how to express.[22]

## Black Power

The televised violence of the big-city riots ignited a political backlash against African Americans. White law-and-order politicians from California to New York were voted into office, in part, by blaming the riots on the liberal social policies of the Johnson administration. In addition, many whites who had been fighting for black civil rights turned away from the movement, some putting their energies

# The Reasons for the Riots

In 1967 the United States was rocked by the worst rioting in American history. In the wake of the riots, President Johnson created a special panel called the National Advisory Commission on Civil Disorders, otherwise known as the Kerner Commission, to investigate the causes of the riots. Reprinted by Peter B. Levy in *America in the Sixties Right, Left, and Center*, the report blames segregation and racism. The report was strongly condemned by many, including presidential candidate Richard Nixon, who was elected in 1968. The Kerner Commission wrote:

"We have visited the riot cities; we have heard many witnesses. . . . [T]his is our basic conclusion: Our nation is moving toward two societies, one black, one white—separate and unequal. . . . Discrimination and segregation have long permeated much of American life; they now threaten the future of every American. . . .

To pursue the present course will involve the continuing polarization of the American community and, ultimately, the destruction of basic democratic values. The alternative is not blind repression or capitulation to lawlessness. It is the realization of common opportunities for all within a single society.

This alternative will require a commitment to national action—compassionate, massive and sustained, backed by the resources of the most powerful and the richest nation on this earth. From every American it will require new attitudes, new understanding, and, above all, new will.

The vital needs of the nation must be met; hard choices must be made, and, if necessary, new taxes enacted. . . .

Segregation and poverty have created in the racial ghetto a destructive environment totally unknown to most white Americans.

What white Americans have never fully understood—but what the Negro can never forget—is that the white society is deeply implicated in the ghetto. White institutions created it, white institutions maintain it, and white society condones it. . . ."

*Police suppress a rioter in Elizabeth City, New Jersey, in 1964.*

*Adults and children raise their fists in the Black Power salute.*

into protesting the escalating war in Vietnam. And the rebellions splintered the black community into those who believed civil rights would only be gained through violence, and the majority who continued to support nonviolent protest.

For many, however, a new sense of black unity was sweeping through the communities. Those who subscribed to this black nationalism, according to Farber, "rejected the idea of a color-blind, melting-pot society and began to fight the legacies of oppression and racism by organizing a multifaceted [many sided] program of . . . Black Power."[24]

The Black Power movement took its inspiration from Malcolm X, who had been assassinated in early 1965. Malcolm X was a leader in the Nation of Islam, an organization that preached black superiority and pride. In his speeches, he stated that black people had been told they were inferior to whites for so long that they believed it themselves. As opposed to King, Malcolm X believed in violence when confronted with racism, saying:

There can be no revolution without bloodshed, and it is nonsense to describe the [nonviolent] civil rights movement in America as a revolution. Revolution is bloody, revolution is hostile, revolution knows no compromise, revolution overturns and destroys everything that gets in its way.[25]

Malcolm X's solution to black problems was not integration but rather a separate and segregated black nation populated only by African Americans.

Malcolm X also believed in Black Power. He stated that African Americans should study their history and explore the accomplishments of the African civilization. An unnamed black civil rights worker spoke of the effects of Malcolm's words:

Sure, King was a significant figure in the civil rights movement, but he was too soft. . . . Malcolm X was more my hero than King was because he touched deep into my heart and soul when he talked about black unity and black pride. . . . If change was to come about, we had to respect ourselves as well as one another and have pride in ourselves as black people. That pride meant to stop thinking of ourselves as inferior. . . . It was only natural that blacks thought of themselves as second-rate because we were treated as such for so long. We also had to stop kissing up to white folks. . . . [T]hey were the cause of all our problems.[26]

As the Black Power movement gained in strength, black civil rights organizations, such as the Student Nonviolent Coordinating Committee (SNCC), that had once been racially integrated were purged of their white members, and new Black Power organizations were formed on hundreds of now-integrated college campuses.

Meanwhile black rhetoric of revolution and violence became more explicit. When SNCC leader H. Rap Brown spoke to student leaders in Cambridge, Maryland, in July 1967, he called for nothing less than violent revolution. Brown told the cheering audience: "Black folk built America [as slaves]. If America don't come around [to our cause] we *going* [to] burn it down, brother. We are going to burn it down if we don't get our share of it. . . . Burn this town down. . . . Don't love [the white man] to death, shoot him to death."[27] Within hours, downtown Cambridge was engulfed in flames started by rioters. After the disturbance ended, politicians called for the arrest of Brown and passed a law—later declared unconstitutional—making it a federal crime to cross state lines with intent to start a riot.

## Black Panthers

Meanwhile in Oakland, California, the police department, in light of growing criticism, issued orders to their officers to stop using inflammatory racial epithets when talking to black people. Oakland's 661-member police force, however, employed only sixteen black officers. Frustrated by what they perceived as continued police brutality, two young black men, Huey Newton and Bobby Seale, decided to form the Black Panther Party for Self-Defense.

The mission of the Panthers was to observe the actions of the Oakland police and to carry guns to defend themselves against police harassment. (At that time it was legal for a person to carry an unconcealed weapon in California.) After studying the legal aspects of police stops and the right to bear arms—and armed with M-1 carbines and .45 caliber automatic pistols—cars full of Black Panthers began to follow police patrols in black neighborhoods.

*Members of the Black Panthers congregate in front of the state capitol building in 1967 in Sacramento, California.*

The Panthers, however, were more than a police watchdog organization. According to Sundiata Acoli, the Black Panther Party

> organized community programs ranging from free breakfast for children, to free health clinics, to rent strikes resulting in tenant ownership of their buildings, to Liberation School for grade-schoolers, to free clothing drives, to campaigns for community control of schools, community control of police, and campaigns to stop drugs, crime, and police murder and brutality in the various Black [neighborhoods] across America.[28]

Along with their perceived powers to stop police harassment, these programs made the Panthers wildly popular with average black citizens. The Panthers also had impeccable taste in fashion that was widely imitated by young men—and some women—in black neighborhoods. Panthers were always seen, according to *Voices of Freedom,* in "black leather jackets, blue shirts, black trousers, and black berets."[29]

While much was made of their fashions in the media, the Black Panthers were a serious organization with strict rules that they expected their members to follow. According to *The Black Panthers Speak*, edited by Philip S. Foner, individual Panthers were not allowed to

> have narcotics or weed in his possession while doing party work [or] be DRUNK while doing daily party work. . . . [In addition no] party member will USE, POINT, or FIRE a weapon of any kind unnecessarily or accidentally at anyone. . . . [and] no party member will commit any crimes against other party members or BLACK people at all, and cannot steal or take from the people, not even a needle or a piece of thread. . . . [Each party member was also told:] Speak politely. . . . Pay fairly for what you buy . . .

# Black Panther Ten-Point Program

The Black Panther Party combined radical rhetoric with free meal and education programs for poor children. In 1967 Panther founders Bobby Seale and Huey Newton spelled out the demands of the party, quoted in *The Black Panthers Speak*, edited by Philip S. Foner. The "Ten-Point Program and Party Platform" states:

"1. *We want freedom. We want power to determine the destiny of our Black Community.* . . .

2. *We want full employment for our people.* . . .
3. *We want an end to the robbery by the white man of our Black Community.*
4. *We want decent housing, fit for shelter of human beings.*

5. *We want education for our people that exposes the true nature of this decadent American society. We want education that teaches us our true history and our role in the present day society.* . . .
6. *We want all Black men to be exempt from military service.*
7. *We want an immediate end to POLICE BRUTALITY and MURDER of black people.* . . .
8. *We want freedom for all black men held in federal, state, county and city prisons and jails.*
9. *We want all black people when brought to trial to be tried in court by a jury of their peer group or people from their black communities as defined by the Constitution of the United States.* . . .
10. *We want land, bread, housing, education, clothing, justice and peace.* . . ."

*Members of the Black Panther Party followed the strict policies of the "Ten-Point Program."*

Return everything you borrow . . . Pay for anything you damage . . . [and do not] hit or swear at people . . . damage property or crops of the poor, oppressed . . . take liberties with women . . . [and if] we ever have to take captives do not ill-treat them.[30]

Whatever the group's rules and goals, police, politicians, and the media were alarmed when they saw heavily armed black men in dark sunglasses patrolling police beats. In order to stop some Panther practices, California lawmakers attempted to pass gun control laws banning possession of automatic weapons. The Panthers made headlines when twenty-six members marched into the state capitol during the debate carrying rifles, pistols, carbines, and bandoliers with live ammunition around their necks. According to the Sterns, "No shots were fired; nobody was even arrested (the weapons were legally carried). But after that astounding piece of theater, *everybody,* knew about the Black Panthers, and everybody knew they meant business."[31]

*Although they were known for their fashionable attire, the Black Panthers were more concerned with serious issues such as racism.*

The lure of the Panthers proved irresistible to disenfranchised young black men in city ghettos, and by 1970 there were Black Panther Party branches in thirty-seven American cities. The radical rhetoric of the party, however, did not go unnoticed by police. In 1969, when one Panther leader advocated the assassination of President Nixon, he was quickly arrested. Several months later, police in Chicago and Los Angeles conducted a series of early morning raids on Black Panther members in their homes, killing two and wounding seven. Within the next several years, authorities arrested, wounded, or killed dozens of Black Panthers, and more than four hundred were indicted on various crimes. Not all of these actions were constitutional, according to a 1969 American Civil Liberties Union (ACLU) report:

> Quite aside from the killing of Panthers and police which we abhor, ACLU affiliates have reported that the style of law enforcement applied to Black Panthers has amounted to provocative and even punitive harassment, defying the constitutional rights of Panthers to make political speeches or distribute political literature.
>
> In San Francisco, Los Angeles, Chicago, Philadelphia and New York, police have made repeated arrests of Panthers for distributing papers without a permit, harassment, interfering with an officer, loitering and disorderly conduct—stemming from incidents where police have challenged Panthers as they attempted to distribute their newspaper or other political materials. Seldom have these charges held up in court, often they have been dropped by the prosecutor prior to trial. . . . We view this style of law enforcement as applied with prejudice to the Panthers, as inflammatory,

and very susceptible to escalation into violent confrontations.[32]

## "The Sound of Young America"

The Black Panthers were popular with a wide segment of young African Americans. News of riots and gun-toting revolutionaries, however, could not obscure other contributions blacks were making to American culture during the 1960s. After the Civil Rights Act was passed in 1964, African Americans began to appear on television in ever-increasing numbers as Hollywood studios began to portray blacks in a more positive light on TV shows.

When Bill Cosby costarred in the Emmy Award–winning secret agent series *I Spy* in 1965, he was the first African American to star in a prime-time TV series. In 1968 Diahann Carroll starred in *Julia* the first series about an African American family, and one that did away with stereotypes and portrayed black characters as living like average middle-class Americans.

While there were only a few black faces on TV, African American singers and musicians were making a huge contribution to American culture. Beginning around 1964, the combination of blues, gospel, and rock known as soul music was quickly becoming the soundtrack of the sixties. Average American citizens—both black and white—were dancing to the songs of Ray Charles, Wilson Pickett, James Brown, and other artists who were selling millions of records. The soul music business was an equal-opportunity employer, and for the first time, dozens of women and "girl groups" were selling as many records as their male counterparts. By 1965 the Supremes were competing with the top-selling Beatles, racking up five consecutive number-one singles, a feat as yet unmatched by any other group.

The Supremes were on the Motown record label, derived from the Motor City, Detroit's nickname, where American cars were built. Motown's founder, Barry Gordy, was an autoworker on the Ford assembly line when he got the idea to start a record company in the late fifties. He signed unknown young black performers, gave them singing and dancing lessons, sent them to charm school to learn poise and fashion, and promoted their music relentlessly.

By the mid-sixties, Motown billed itself as "the Sound of Young America."[33] Motown artists such as Marvin Gaye, Smokey Robinson, Mary Wells, Stevie Wonder, the Four Tops, and the Temptations sold millions of records to white and black teenagers. Soul artists appeared on national television shows, their music was played on white-owned rock radio stations, and their message crossed color lines, integrating American culture in profound and long-lasting ways.

## Say It Loud!

Black artists who recorded for other labels were also extremely popular. Otis Redding, Wilson Pickett, and others followed Motown's success

*The look and the sound of the girl group the Supremes attracted both white and black audiences.*

in "crossing over" to white audiences. And some hit soul songs contained a strong Black Power message. James Brown's 1968 hit "Say It Loud—I'm Black and I'm Proud" became an anthem in African American neighborhoods. And perhaps no one demanded recognition better than that lady of soul Aretha Franklin, the daughter of a Baptist minister, whose song "Respect" became a lasting icon of the sixties.

In *She's a Rebel*, Gillian G. Gaar writes about the social implications of the songs made popular while inner cities were in turmoil:

> "Respect" hit a potent nerve in 1967. . . . Riots broke out in the black neighborhoods of several cities across America throughout the summer; [Martha and] the Vandellas were performing their "inflammatory" number "Dancing in the Streets" in Detroit on the very night a four-day riot was sparked off. . . . "Newspapers, periodicals and television commentators pondered the question of 'Why?' as Aretha Franklin spelled it all out in one word, R-E-S-P-E-C-T!" wrote Phyl Garland in *The Soul Scene*. . . . But "Respect's" broad appeal was also due to the fact that the song could be read in a number of different

ways. "It could be a racial situation, it could be a political situation, it could be just the man-woman situation," Tom Dowd, the recording engineer for the song, told *Rolling Stone*, adding, "Anybody could identify with it. It cut a lot of ground."[34]

## Negative and Positive

The popularity of soul music was just one positive factor for African Americans in the sixties. After centuries of discrimination and racism, American society began to slowly change as civil rights and voting rights were enshrined in American law. It was also a time of tragedy as popular leaders such as Martin Luther King, Malcolm X, and others fell to assassins' bullets while black neighborhoods erupted in flames. Although at times the negative seemed to dominate headlines, the overall lasting impact of the sixties had many positive features. Discrimination was outlawed, and the profound speeches of Dr. King—along with the soaring harmonies of the soul groups—helped put into words the respect and dignity that America owed to its black citizens.

# Counterculture

At the beginning of the 1960s, American culture dominated the free world. It was the dawn of the space age with more advanced American rockets soaring off into the sky every year and the first man landing on the moon in 1969. America was also the most powerful country in the world, with the U.S. military keeping the world free from communist domination. Fast cars, fast food, instant suburbs, and the American way of life were sold to the rest of the world on television, in magazines, and in the movies.

The baby boomers were growing up fast, their tastes and styles dominating, as only teenagers can, the daily lives of their parents. As the richest and best-educated generation in history, they were destined to inherit the American prosperity and culture their parents had worked so hard to build. It was a culture that honored the values of capitalism, clean living, patriotism, and unquestioned respect for authority.

No social scientist studying the United States in 1962, however, could have predicted the stunning turn American culture would take within the next ten years. It would have been inconceivable for anyone to imagine early in the decade that a large majority of America's children would radically rebuff the cherished values of their parents. They would form a new, entirely different culture that rejected almost everything their parents held dear. These idealistic people were antiwar, valued mind expansion via drug use, and promoted sexual freedom.

Their culture was the exact opposite of, or counter to, the prevailing culture, and they quickly became known as the counterculture. Their values continued to remain a part of society for decades in areas such as music, ecology, health food, women's rights, and gay rights.

## A Beat Beginning

Although the 1950s are portrayed as an era of strict conformity, in big cities such as New York there were a few artists, poets, and musicians who defied social norms and became the founders of the hippie generation. Writers such as Jack Kerouac and William Burroughs, poets like Allen Ginsburg, artists such as Jackson Pollock, and black jazz musicians such as Charlie "Bird" Parker, defied social convention and peppered the fifties landscape with exciting and outrageous works of art. Jack Kerouac, in particular, brought bohemian consciousness to popular American culture with his best-selling book *On the Road*. The book, as described on its cover, "is a saga of youth adrift in America, traveling by highways, exploring the midnight streets of the cities, learning the vast expanse of the land, passionately searching for their country and themselves."[35]

The popularity of *On the Road* led thousands of teenagers to take to the highways. The destination for many was the City on the Bay, San Francisco, California. By the early sixties, tens of thousands of young people were attracted to the bohemian lifestyle in dozens of big city neighborhoods across the country. They called themselves beats or beatniks, a term taken from black slang used to describe someone who was beaten down, but later modified to also mean beatific, or at peace. Most beatniks wrote poetry, drank strong coffee and cheap wine, smoked marijuana, and listened to jazz music while rejecting traditional American values. Beatnik philosophies are explained by Martin A. Lee and Bruce Shlain in *Acid Dreams:*

> The beats had nothing but contempt for the strictures of a society . . . fixated on success, cleanliness, and material possession. Whatever the mainstream tried to conceal, denigrate, or otherwise purge from experience, the beats flaunted. Their hunger for new sensations led them to seek transcendence through jazz, marijuana, Buddhist meditation, and the frenetic pace of the hip life style.[36]

By 1960 the North Beach neighborhood of San Francisco was a swirling parade of beret-wearing beatnik characters strumming guitars, reading poetry, and making paintings.

*Jack Kerouac's best-selling novel,* On the Road, *led thousands of American youths to discover beatnik philosophies.*

*Coffeehouses like this one in New York City attracted many in the beatnik culture who found new freedoms of expression in poetry and folk music.*

## Flamboyant Behavior

North Beach in the early sixties was also a center for folk musicians who were melding white country ballads with black-inspired blues into a new form called folk music. They played at small coffeehouses and clubs with names such as the "hungry i." These clubs often attracted middle-class teens who had the money and education to reject, with few consequences, America's consumer-oriented society. And alienation was rampant, according to Paul Kantner of the band Jefferson Airplane:

I thought I was either going to have to commit suicide or become a bank robber . . . I got into folk music and it probably saved my life. . . . San Francisco has always held a peculiar fascination for people who live outside the pale. . . . It was like Oz for us, a hedonistic place which gave you the opportunity to be rather flamboyant and extreme in your behavior. [The folk scene] was a group of well-educated children breaking out of binds set for them that didn't really apply. . . . And almost, in their own way, throwing themselves into a fire of unknown origin.[37]

Much of the flamboyant behavior described by Kantner was the result of alcohol and drugs. While some jazz musicians had been using marijuana—and heroin—for decades, a new drug, LSD, whose scientific name lysergic acid diethylamide gave it its street name "acid," was making its way onto the scene. LSD was so powerful and so potent that it changed its users in profound ways, causing many to believe they had seen God or the devil, or witnessed the creation of the universe.

LSD was originally used in top-secret experiments by CIA agents who gave it to unknowing test subjects in the 1950s. The CIA spent millions of dollars—and dosed thousands of people—in order to determine LSD's use as a brainwashing agent against enemy spies. When the drug proved too unpredictable for such purposes, government researchers began giving LSD to college students, who were paid $75 to report on the drug's effects.

One of those students was Ken Kesey, a brawny, curly-haired farm boy from Oregon. Kesey, who was attending Stanford University in Palo Alto on a creative writing fellowship, began to augment his income as a night attendant at a local veterans' hospital. There he discovered a wide array of psychedelic drugs, including LSD and mescaline, stocked in the medicine cabinet in the psychiatric ward, where they were used for research into mental illness.

Kesey often spent the late-night hours on his job high on LSD, observing the inmates of the ward. He later said: "Before I took drugs . . . I didn't know why the guys in the psycho ward at the VA Hospital were there. I didn't understand them. After I took LSD, suddenly I saw it. I saw it all. I listened to them and watched them, and I saw that what they were saying and doing was not so crazy after all."[38]

Inspired by the antics of the men in the ward where he worked, Kesey wrote a book called *One Flew Over the Cuckoo's Nest*, which quickly became a best-seller. With the profits from the book, Kesey bought a cottage in La Honda, outside Palo Alto, and began giving LSD to writers, artists, musicians, and even members of the Hell's Angels motorcycle club. In *Beneath the Diamond Sky: Haight-Ashbury 1965–1970*, Barney Hoskyns explains what happened next:

> Isolated within six acres and a mountain creek, they were free to pursue their chemical experiments out of eyesight and earshot, wiring up equipment and speakers in the house and in the redwoods surrounding it so they could groove to [jazz artist] Rahsaan Roland Kirk records while chopping wood.

*Author Ken Kesey was inspired to write the novel* One Flew Over the Cuckoo's Nest *while working in a psychiatric hospital high on LSD.*

Everything now came down to the crucial experience of LSD, which made it impossible to live by the straight world's games. When Kesey's tough, larger-than-life pal Ken Babbs returned from active duty as a helicopter pilot in Vietnam, the [group known as the] Merry Pranksters [was] born, and things became rapidly more intense and maniacal. The Pranksters bought a 1939 International Harvester school bus . . . and daubed it with psychedelic swirls and patterns and endowed it with intense spiritual significance. . . . The Pranksters embarked in the summer of 1964 on an insane, sleepless, paranoid odyssey that took them all the way through the desert of the Southwest to Texas to New Orleans and then up to New York City . . . all the while filming their escapades and encounters with straight America. At the rear of the bus hung a sign: CAUTION: WEIRD LOAD; at the front, its destination board read: FURTHER.[39]

## Turning On, Tuning In, and Dropping Out

Kesey was not the only person wishing to spread the message of LSD. Timothy Leary, a clinical psychology professor at Harvard University in Massachusetts, had begun taking psychedelic mushrooms in the early sixties. In his book *The Politics of Ecstasy*, Leary describes

*Timothy Leary was fired from Harvard for giving psilocybin mushrooms to students who volunteered for his experiments.*

# Timothy Leary's Message

Timothy Leary was a flamboyant spokesman for the counterculture whose drug-induced pronouncements often captured headlines. In his book *The Politics of Ecstasy*, Leary explains what he means when he says: Tune in. Turn on. Drop out.

*Turning On*
By turning on I mean get in touch, first of all, with your sense organs. . . . Get in touch with your cellular wisdom. Get in touch with the universe within. The only way out is in [to your mind]. And the way to find the wisdom within is to turn on.

*Tuning In*
By tune in I mean harness your internal revelations to the external world around you. I am not suggesting that we find a desert island and curl up under a palm tree and take LSD and study our navels. As I look around at the people who have taken LSD, far from being inactive, lazy, or passive, I see them in

every walk of life and in every age group, struggling to express what they're learning. The hippie movement, the psychedelic style, involves a revolution in our concepts of art and creativity which is occurring right before our eyes.

*Dropping Out . . .*
Find the wisdom within, give up in a new way, but above all, detach yourself. Unhook the ambitions and the symbolic tribes and the mental connections which keep you addicted and tied to the immediate [capitalistic] game.

Is our American society so insecure that it cannot tolerate our young people taking a year or two off, growing beards, wandering around the country, fooling with new forms of consciousness? This is one of the oldest traditions in civilized society. Take a voyage! Take the adventure! Before you settle down to the tribal game, try out self-exile. You're coming back will be much enriched."

the results as "the deepest religious experience of my life."[40]

Leary was fired from Harvard in 1963 for giving hallucinogenic psilocybin mushrooms to hundreds of volunteer students. After his dismissal, he continued to experiment with peyote, marijuana, mescaline, and LSD. Astounded by the effects of these drugs, Leary started a private research group called the International Foundation for Internal Freedom (IFIF) and set up a psychedelic study center in a 64-room mansion on a 4,000-acre estate in Millbrook, New York, donated by multimillionaire William Hitchcock, heir to the Gulf Oil fortune.

Leary believed that LSD could positively change the human race and began preaching his message in magazines and on television. He

told Americans that they should "Turn on. Tune in. Drop out."[41] Although his ideas were eventually embraced by millions, Leary advocated that people should only take LSD under controlled conditions with guides to help them through the acid "trip."

Meanwhile on the West Coast, Kesey had similar revelations and, much to the dismay of researchers like Leary, began to hand out acid to everyone and anyone. The Merry Pranksters pursued their quest with a passionate enthusiasm. In 1965 LSD was still legal, and Kesey held a series of "acid tests"—huge parties where LSD was given to thousands of people, who decorated their bodies with Day-Glo paint, watched protoplasmic light shows, and danced all night long to the psychedelic rock of

# Sixties Music

Sixties rock-and-roll music was one of the guiding forces of the counterculture movement. Over 73 million people watched the Beatles on the *Ed Sullivan Show* in 1964, and the group instantly inspired millions of teens to grow long hair and learn to play guitars and drums. The Beatles also spawned hundreds of imitators, who began to fill the radio waves with unique and innovative songs filled with harmony and raw musical talent.

At the same time, Bob Dylan was writing dozens of songs with lyrical poetry often scornful of racism, poverty, war, and other social problems. Dylan's songs became anthems of the antiwar movement, and when he sang on his 1965 album *Blonde on Blonde* that "everybody must get stoned," for the first time drug use was openly encouraged in the mass media.

In the Bay Area, folk and blues musicians took LSD, picked up electric guitars, and invented the San Francisco sound. They played at various concerts where psychedelic light shows flashed and pulsated along with the music. The Grateful Dead, Jefferson Airplane, Quicksilver Messenger Service, and Janis Joplin's Big Brother and the Holding Company played free concerts in Golden Gate Park almost every month. The hippies in the Haight were exposed to a wide variety of musical styles because rock promoter Bill Graham paired psychedelic bands with African American blues greats such as John Lee Hooker and B.B. King, along with Mexican American groups such as Santana.

The music of the counterculture reached its peak of popularity in August 1969 when more than 500,000 rock fans descended on the town of Bethel, New York, for the Woodstock Arts and Crafts Festival, which featured dozens of the sixties' best-selling bands.

*Common themes in musician Bob Dylan's work include war, poverty, and racism.*

*The Merry Pranksters decorate a bus with psychedelic patterns.*

the Grateful Dead and other bands. The so-called Trips Festivals continued for several years (although LSD was outlawed in 1966), and LSD use spread across America. Meanwhile in San Francisco, the acid heads moved to a working-class neighborhood near Golden Gate Park called Haight-Ashbury where, according to Lee and Shlain, "the cultural rebellion fueled by LSD happened so vividly and with such intensity that it attracted worldwide attention."[42]

LSD experiences often caused users to experience intense feelings of love for others. As a result, the summer of 1967 was referred to by many as the Summer of Love. By July of that year, hippie neighborhoods modeled on Haight-Ashbury began to pop up in every major American city from the Coventry area of Cleveland, Ohio, to the East Village in New York. In college towns such as Eugene, Oregon, and Cornell, New York, acid-dropping hippies soon began to outnumber average citizens.

Within a few years, an estimated 6 million people, from junior high school students to Hollywood movie stars, had experimented with LSD and other psychoactive drugs. Farber describes the result of this massive uncontrolled drug experiment:

The counterculture of Haight-Ashbury, as well as other freak enclaves, grew as acid use spread. . . . [Initiates to LSD] then worked/played at turning their streets into expressions of their acid dreams. Going by

*A hippie expresses his counter-culture ideals in New York City in 1968.*

their acid names—Wildflower, Bear, Mountain Girl, Cowboy—wearing their archetypal acid clothes—buckskin, Hindu robes, rainbow-colored tie-dyed ensembles—stripped down from the materialist "uptight" paraphernalia of society—barefoot, hair flying, undergarments thrown away—they painted and chalked, rang bells and chanted mantras, and, yes, wore flowers in their hair. Influenced by acid's reality-bending effects, they embraced a world without rules in which the old "control systems" of science and reason squared off against the "direct spinal language" of magic and mysticism.

The freaks' public embrace of illegal drugs like marijuana and LSD was sufficient to infuriate—and scare—most Americans. "Turned-on" youths' flouting of sexual conventions widened the gulf and increased the stakes. In a nation where, as late as 1969, more than two-thirds of all people believed that premarital sex of any kind was wrong, the hippies anthem of "Free Love!" resounded, as it was meant to, as a war cry.[43]

## Hippie Backlash

This kaleidoscopic psychedelic experiment did not go unnoticed by the media. Nearly every week, a major magazine such as *Time*, or *Newsweek* featured stories on different aspects of the hippie revolution. Local newspapers and magazines in almost every city also published stories on the counterculture phenomenon that seemed to burst into public consciousness virtually overnight. These stories were accompanied by dancing

## The Sexual Revolution

Suburban parents may not have understood the implications of the widespread use of LSD, but they could not ignore the new message of sexual freedom preached by those in the counterculture. In the 1950s, the topic of sex was rarely mentioned and children were taught that sexual abstinence was mandatory until marriage. In the 1960s, however, sexual inhibitions were considerably loosened by drugs. The birth control pill had been introduced in the early sixties, and by mid-decade over 6 million American women were on the pill. By providing nearly 100 percent protection from pregnancy, the pill freed women, for the first time in history, from the fear of unwanted pregnancy. In this era before AIDS, women were suddenly free to join men in widespread sexual experimentation. The results of this phenomenon are explored in *The Times Were a Changin',* edited by Irwin and Debi Unger.

"The Pill, announced with little fanfare in 1960, had ended the fear of pregnancy; penicillin had diminished fear of [sexually transmitted} disease. Sex . . . in any form, was considered good; denial was bad. The new sexual liberation movement soon spread beyond youthful flower-child dropouts. All through middle-class and working-class America ran a new current of permissiveness. The magazine and TV commentators began to report 'wife-swapping' as the latest suburban di-

version. Divorce rates soared as both men and women, hitherto resigned to sexual disappointments, sought erotic adventure and fulfillment outside of marriage. The federal courts, in the name of the First Amendment rights to free speech, began to provide protection to erotic and even pornographic publications. The movie industry moved with the tide to allow mature audiences to be exposed to bad language and nudity."

*With the advent of the birth control pill, many women enjoyed sexual freedom without the worry of pregnancy.*

images of young hippies dressed in psyche-delic colors.

The often fanciful hippie stories in the media quickly garnered the attention of millions of young adults who were beginning to enter the rebellious phase of their teenage lives. With a ready-made way to reject their parents' values, it was not long before flowing hair, bells, beads, and other hippie garb began appearing in millions of suburban homes. Many of these teens soon took to the road, hitchhiking, driving, or flying off to the hippie wonderlands they saw portrayed in the media.

While attracting many positive and well-meaning people, by the late sixties hippie neighborhoods had also became magnets for troubled young runaways. These distressed teens were easy prey for older, more sophisticated adults who might use them sexually or encourage them to sell drugs. Farber describes some of the troubled people in Haight-Ashbury:

> According to one scholarly study, by 1968 about 15 percent of the young people drawn to the Haight were psychotics and religious obsessives, and about 45 percent were dropouts, lowlifes, and hard livers, most of them young men looking to find sex and get stoned as often as possible. A minority of true-believing freaks tried to build their alternative community in what was fast becoming an out-of-control mess in which no one felt they had the right or the authority—"do your own thing" being the watchword of the community's faith—to tell the crazies and heroin addicts and the violent criminals to go away.[44]

## Bad Trips

LSD is a powerful drug that induces a kind of artificial psychosis that some are better able to manage than others—and the LSD available in the mid-sixties was three to ten times more potent than the LSD that was available on the streets in later years. The power of the drug was made obvious by the terms people use to describe it, such as "mind blowing" and "dynamite." Acid gurus such as Timothy Leary recommended that LSD be taken in a peaceful and controlled setting. Unfortunately, the often mean streets of hippie neighborhoods were not ideal places to experiment with such a mind-blowing drug.

It was well known, even to the original hippies in Haight-Ashbury, that LSD users could have "bad trips," full of paranoia, terror, and dark thoughts of "never coming down" to regain sanity. These usually occurred several hours into the LSD trip and evaporated for most people as the drug wore off. In 1966, however, William Frosch, a psychiatrist working at New York's Bellevue Hospital, testified before a Senate subcommittee that about seven out of a thousand people who took LSD had what was called a "psychotic episode" requiring hospital treatment and psychiatric attention. Almost every person who had such an episode had a previous history of psychiatric problems. Unfortunately, with the drug being handed out on street corners across America, there was no way to keep LSD out of the hands of people who were psychologically unbalanced. Those who "never came down" often ended up living on the streets of hippie neighborhoods, sleeping in parks, eating from Dumpsters, and numbing themselves with liquor or dangerous drugs.

This mix of runaways, thrill seekers, and hardened felons quickly destroyed the dreams of the original peace-loving hippies by the late sixties. In the summer of 1967 alone, a community of about seven thousand original hippies in Haight-Ashbury was overwhelmed by about seventy-five thousand hippie "wanna-bes" who had little money, nowhere to live, nothing to eat, and no way to earn a living. Behind them followed the national and international news media along with tourists, some who rode on huge buses down Haight Street, snapping pictures of children standing on street corners, as if the hippies were exhibits in a museum.

## Life in the Paisley Ghetto

While some may have laughed at hippie antics, authorities were not amused. Timothy Leary was arrested with a tiny amount of marijuana and given a thirty-year prison term of which he served nearly seven years. Federal law enforcement and tax agencies such as the FBI, CIA, Internal Revenue Service (IRS), and Customs Department began cracking down on LSD dealers. On October 6, 1966, the state of California made LSD illegal, and the federal government quickly followed suit. Political organizers in Haight-Ashbury put together the Love Pageant Rally to mark the end of the legal LSD era. Like most other events in Haight-Ashbury, the party ended with a free concert by the Grateful Dead and other bands.

In January 1967 leaders of the Love Pageant decided to hold an even bigger rally called the Human Be-In—a Gathering of the Tribes, which would highlight the idealistic beliefs of the hippie revolution. Rather than hold up protest signs and march against the establishment, the Human Be-In was meant to bring together left-wing political radicals, apolitical street hippies, and just plain people who wanted

to celebrate a day in the sun. In his book *Do It!* antiwar leader Jerry Rubin describes the Be-In:

> Rock music. Grass. Sun. Beautiful bodies. Paint. Ecstasy. Rainbows. No strangers! Everybody smiling. *No picket signs or political banners.* Our nakedness was our picket sign. . . .

> We were cowboys and Indians, pirates, kings, gypsies and Greeks. It was a panorama of history. The rock bands created a tribal, animal energy. We were a religion, a family, a culture, with our own music, our own dress, our own human relationships, our own stimulants, our own media. And we believed that our energy *would turn on the world*. All that energy in one place at one time was the Atom Bomb explosion of the youth culture.

> The Be-In: the new medium of human relations. A magnet drawing together all the freaky, hip, unhappy, young, happy, curious, criminal, gentle, alienated, weird, frustrated, far-out, artistic, lonely, lovely people to the same place at the same time. We could see one another, touch one another and realize that *we* were not *alone*. All the rebellion was reaffirmed.[45]

## The Diggers

Although some leaders such as Timothy Leary encouraged teens to drop out, there were people on the streets of Haight-Ashbury who had to deal with those unsophisticated hordes of unemployed young adults who were descending on San Francisco every day. The most famous of these groups was the Diggers, who distributed free food to homeless teenagers in Golden Gate Park every afternoon.

*A member of the Diggers serves a bowl of soup in Golden Gate Park.*

The Diggers took their name from a seventeenth-century English political movement that illegally occupied farmland in Surrey. Utilizing this annexed land, the Diggers fed themselves and the poor in order to protest high food prices. The San Francisco Diggers fed poor hippies by searching through garbage

Dumpsters behind grocery stores and restaurants for discarded food. They also took scraps and spoils from butchers and vegetable distributors. Beginning at eight every morning, the Diggers would boil down chickens and turkeys to make broth for a stew. At 4 P.M. they would go to the panhandle of Golden Gate Park, a narrow strip of land that borders the Haight-Ashbury neighborhood, and give the food away. According to the autobiography *Ringolevio* by Digger founder Emmett Grogan, the Diggers announced their intentions with fliers that read: "FREE FOOD/GOOD HOT STEW. . . . BRING A BOWL AND SPOON TO THE PANHANDLE AT ASHBURY STREET 4:00PM. . . . FREE FOOD *EVERYDAY* FREE FOOD/IT'S FREE BECAUSE IT'S YOURS!"[46]

As many as five hundred people would show up for daily Digger dinners, many with bowls and spoons tied to their belts. The organization, however, was dead-set against capitalism, and when diners offered money for the food, Diggers would burn the bills before an amazed crowd. The Diggers later rented a six-car garage and set up a free store to give away clothing and other items, many of which were stolen.

The Diggers Archive website reports on the many activities of the group that spread far beyond the Haight-Ashbury community:

> The Diggers coined various slogans that worked their way into the counterculture and even into the larger society—"Do your own thing" and "Today is the first day of the rest of your life" being the most recognizable. The Diggers, at the nexus of the emerging underground, were the progenitors of many new (or newly discovered) ideas such as baking whole wheat bread (made famous through the popular Free Digger Bread that was baked in one- and two-pound coffee cans at the Free Bakery); the first Free Medical Clinic, which inspired the founding of the Haight-Ashbury Free Medical Clinic; [tie]-dyed clothing; and communal celebrations of natural planetary events, such as the Solstices and Equinoxes.[47]

While the Diggers tried to remain true to their anticapitalist vision of a free world, by 1968 it was obvious that the hippie movement had run its course. And Haight-Ashbury had been transformed into a dangerous tourist trap, as the Sterns explain:

> The beautiful [hippie] ideal turned into a circus. Dozens of souvenir stores, head shops, and junk-food places opened on Haight Street to serve the tourists. Mellowness and good vibes grew scarce in a neighborhood ever more crowded with hustlers, sex perverts, gawking tourists, dealers on a violence trip, needle freaks shooting speed.[48]

## The Commune Movement

As the hippie dream turned into a nightmare in some cities, thousands of people decided to move to the country. Some moved together in groups to form small rural societies known as communes, where the property was shared by everybody and whose members shared common interests, work, and income.

The trickle of people that started leaving the cities for communes around 1965 turned into a flood by 1969. The Sterns describe the commune movement:

> The goal of those who split were these: to groove on nature; to grow their own grass; to bake their own bread; to seize cosmic truth by getting *real*, slopping hogs, planting beans, and throwing clay pots. The more primitive, the better.
>
> The main thing country hippies sought was innocence. Hippie logic presumed that innocence was good. From the beginning, acid trips were marketed as a greater way to sweep your mind clean in order to rediscover the glory of being simple. . . .

Although virtually all of them were Caucasian, hippies relished their romantic self-image as nouveau [Native Americans], living in harmony with the universe, fighting against the white man's perverted society of pollution, war, and greed. Country paradise, hippie style, was like a version of Indian life from some old Hollywood movie, in which the long-haired tribesman in buckskin fringe sit around their tepees smoking pipes, beating tom-toms, and speaking in [self-important] homilies, while the [women] . . . tend the babies and make dinner in elegantly primitive huts.[49]

By the end of the 1960s, there were more than two thousand communes scattered across the United States, and perhaps several hundred thousand people living on some sort of commune, each having an estimated twenty to fifty people. According to Timothy Miller in *The 60s Communes:*

> Once it got well started, about 1968, the communal stream became a torrent as the alienated young banded together in thousands of places, likely and unlikely, urban and rural. Media publicity had a good deal to do with it. The early coverage of the new-generation communes tended to be in specialized publications and the underground press, which by 1968 was thriving in hundreds of American cities and towns. Soon, however, the colorful communes

*A group of women prepares a salad in the kitchen tent at a commune.*

were featured in all the mass print media—daily newspapers, *Time*, and *Newsweek*, and *Life*, rural weeklies, and just about every other venue. Reporters and readers alike were fascinated with, and often are outraged by, these strange-looking eccentrics who had suddenly taken up residence in their midst. . . . Sensationalism, then as now, was the order of the day for any self-respecting news outlet; so much of the coverage focused on nudity and drug use, real or rumored—and thus helped to feed the local hostility towards communes that broke out so often. . . .[50]

As the news media publicized the commune movement, these small farms in the country were overwhelmed with uninvited guests. In July 1969 *Life* published an article about a commune in Oregon, showing pictures of people living in tepees and bathing nude in a creek. Within weeks, hundreds of teenagers flocked to the farm and the commune quickly failed under the strain.

Many of those arriving daily at these new communes had grown up as pampered middle-class children who were unfamiliar with the backbreaking work of farming with primitive tools and equipment. Tilling the soil, planting, weeding, cutting wood for heat, building outhouses and other buildings, maintaining automobiles, and caring for livestock proved to be too great a strain for many, and some communes failed within their first year. And in the days before women's liberation, women were still generally assigned the traditional tasks of sewing, cooking, cleaning, and child care. Living in large groups and sharing money and possessions were also sources of friction to those raised in the suburbs.

Some communes were victims of their own success. The Drop City commune in Colorado attracted so many people that it was hard to maintain decent living conditions, as Miller writes:

The entire commune of forty (give or take a few) people and its constant stream of visitors somehow got by on food stamps and a sporadic income that seldom exceeded a $100 a month. If one was simply marking time and interested in having fun, Drop City was a very economical way to do it. But fun came at a certain price. The kitchen was filthy, and there was no soap because money was short. Hepatitis had recently swept through the commune, and still no one was motivated enough to see that soap was made available. Sleeping quarters were seriously overcrowded. The outhouse was filled to overflowing, and there was no lime to sterilize it. In 1970 Drop City had become . . . a laboratory dedicated to a totally minimal existence.[51]

## The Dream is Over

By 1970, for many the counterculture dreams of peace and love had been shattered. In later years, many would look back on the sixties and find fault with the people who believed they could so easily change the world. In the context of the events that were dominating the sixties, however, it may be easier to understand the movement.

The culture of the United States in the 1960s was in chaos for much of the decade. A bloody war raged in Vietnam that was opposed by millions of people. Meanwhile, black neighborhoods across the country were burned in anger to protest racism. Idealistic young leaders such as John Kennedy, Robert Kennedy, and Martin Luther King Jr. were gunned down in their prime before their collective vision of a better society could take hold. At the same time, millions of middle-class children were becoming young adults, and the streets were flooded with a new drug that caused many people to lose their inhibitions and search for a different way of life.

The convergence of the prosperous baby boom, the civil rights movement, the Vietnam War, and widespread use of LSD was an unlikely historical coincidence. And yet those incidents that happened for a very short time so long ago are still vividly remembered by some today. For a brief several years, millions of people believed they could positively expand their minds, spread peace and love throughout the human race, and save the world by renouncing materialism. As Jerry Garcia, lead guitarist and founding member of the Grateful Dead, stated:

There was a moment when there was a vision; there was a very wonderful vision, seeing it had to do with everybody acting in good faith, it had to do with everybody behaving right. It was really a moment, it was like a breath there for a moment, it was like an open door, Ohh look [at how great it can be], you know. . . .[52]

# The Soldiers

**CHAPTER 4**

During the sixties era of psychedelic drugs and free love, the United States was also waging a bloody war in Vietnam—the longest and most costly war in American history. Some of the young men wandering around hippie neighborhoods and experimenting with drugs were "dodging" the draft—that is, hiding out from authorities who wanted to induct them into the army. Almost all of those in the counterculture opposed the war.

In spite of the protests against the draft and the antiwar sentiment, a full two-thirds of the soldiers who went to Vietnam—2 million men—were volunteers. In addition, eleven thousand women volunteered for military service. Many of these men and women joined the military because they had limited options and wanted to serve their country and see the world. Those who served in Vietnam were also young, with an average age of nineteen. (The average age of those who fought in World War II was twenty-six.) Almost all of those killed and wounded were under the age of thirty.

Military benefits that offered low-cost mortgages or paid for a college education after service also attracted people of lesser means. As a result, nearly 80 percent of soldiers in the 1960s came from poor, inner-city, or working-class backgrounds. Historian Chris Appey explains why many of these young men were inspired to enlist: "The draft was on their necks, school was a boring hassle, jobs all seemed dead end, family life was becoming unbearable, conflicts with authorities were turning serious and dangerous."[53]

## Trust in the Government

While the antiwar movement made headlines throughout the sixties, few Americans questioned the morality of the war until late in the decade. Fighting communism across the globe had been accepted American military policy since World War II, and Vietnam was just another country facing a communist threat. When the war began, the U.S. Congress almost unanimously supported President Johnson's actions

*Thousands of Marines land in Chu Lai, South Vietnam, in 1965.*

against the North Vietnamese; however, most Americans had little information about Vietnam or the growing conflict from which to draw an opinion. They were repeatedly assured that the war would be over quickly and the United States would be victorious.

Jan Barry served in the army from 1962 to 1965 and spent ten months in Vietnam. In *Winter Soldiers* by Richard Stacewicz, Barry describes the trust average citizens put in the government in the early sixties:

> One of the things that is so difficult to describe after [what happened in] the late 1960s is what it was like before that time.... when I graduated from high school in 1961, we had no idea you could question anything. No matter what the government did, there wasn't even the thought that you could question whatever it was.[54]

Family tradition was another factor for those who joined the military. A large majority of the baby boomers were born to Americans who had served in World War II. When these children were growing up it, was not unusual for them to hear their relatives tell war stories. Army veteran Jack McClosky, who spent 1966 in Vietnam, explains:

> Everybody in my neighborhood, all my relatives, all my uncles, my father, everybody was in the military during the Second World War. My uncle Danny was a career Marine. He had lots of stories of what it was like. My uncle Joe . . . was a machine gunner in the Army. My father was in the merchant marine. My uncle Ray was an officer in the Army. My uncle Bobby was in the Navy with the Pacific fleet. My uncle Bill was in the Marines. Every uncle I could think of—all of them had military backgrounds.

Part of my upbringing is that if you were a male, there was an obligation—not just to get out of the ghetto, but as part of a way of life— that you went into the service. This was part of becoming a man. It was part of the transference from adolescence to adulthood.[55]

## Basic Training

For those following in the footsteps of their fathers and uncles, the first days of Vietnam-era military service had changed little since the 1940s. Young men gathered with a group of about a hundred other enlistees at a local bus or train station. Each was allowed one suitcase and most were accompanied by their parents, wives, or girlfriends.

Fresh recruits were often shipped to boot camp far from home—men from the North were sent to bases in Georgia and southerners were sent to New Jersey. Few recruits were prepared for the harsh treatment they would receive from the moment they rolled into camp. John Lundquist, who wanted to be a marine since he was a young boy, describes his first minutes in the military:

> I get off the bus in boot camp. The staff sergeant gets on the bus and says we have a minute to get off the bus, "Five seconds are over; now move." Everybody starts scrambling. [The sergeant] already grabbed the first guy by the hair and threw him out the door. [We get in line] and the guy next to me started picking his nose. So he [the sergeant] walked up and decked the guy. He knocked him out. . . . I didn't move a muscle. He was waiting for me to move a muscle because he was going to deck me too. I didn't say nothing. I didn't do nothing. I didn't move. . . . I

*Army recruits participate in rigorous physical conditioning at Fort Dix in New Jersey.*

knew [at that moment] I had messed up and it was too late. Then I also at the same time thought. . . . I'm married; my wife is pregnant; I'm making $96 a month; and I'm going to Vietnam. I knew it wouldn't do any good to resist. I'm stuck.[56]

After arrival, new recruits received half-inch crew cuts, were vaccinated by doctors with inch-long needles, and were issued ill-fitting uniforms. The recruits gave up their identities for a rank and serial number. Their first days in boot camp were filled with mind-numbing and exhausting regimens of calisthenics, marching at 128 steps per minute, practicing with weapons, and performing tedious tasks in the kitchens, motor pools, and elsewhere. Sleep was limited to

about four hours per night. Young men who had gone to college had a particularly difficult time adjusting to this new world of tough-talking men and monotonous physical drudgery.

Basic training was more than physical exercise. Recruits were controlled mentally and emotionally so that they would not question the orders of the officers. David Ewing, who joined the army in the late sixties, explains his experiences in basic training:

People were psychologically broken very, very quickly. People who are ungainly, uncoordinated, or nerds were just brutally dealt with by the drill sergeants. A lot of young people were broken by the experience. One guy in my company committed

Racism was a fact of life in the military just as it was in civilian life during the 1960s. According to *A Nation Divided* by Clark Dougan and Samuel Lipsman:

"At Camp Lejeune, home of about 30,000 marines, 70 percent of them Vietnam veterans, a clash in July 1969 between blacks and whites left one corporal dead and at least 15 others wounded. . . . The Department of the Army report later admitted that the army had 'a race problem of serious proportions both in the continental United States and overseas' and that 'Negro soldiers seem to have lost faith in the Army.'

Grievances of blacks in the armed forces were often justified. While they made up nearly 10 percent of all army personnel, they constituted only 3.4 percent of the officer corps and a bare 0.6 percent of officers ranking colonel or above. Arrested black soldiers were held in pretrial confinement an average of five days longer than whites. . . . Fifty percent of all soldiers held in confinement . . . were black. Moreover, punitive discharges as a result of courts-martial were given to blacks 33 percent more often than whites, and when sentenced to hard labor, the average black was given a full year longer than a white. So bad had racial tensions become that on some bases blacks began to wage a guerrilla war against whites. A barracks area at Fort Benning, Georgia, known as Kelley Hill, was the scene of many nighttime attacks upon white soldiers."

suicide, hanged himself in the barracks on the weekend. I was 20. I was one of the oldest people, certainly the most mature of pretty much anybody.

It was a crazy scene in the military. It's like living with 20 armed ten-year-olds or sixteen-year-olds. There's all this emotional range of craziness and very immature people with access to big weapons. . . .

Part of the training is not to permit you to sleep. It's important to mold people. If you don't let them sleep, it breaks their resistance. I hadn't slept in about six weeks. I was really tired.[57]

## The Officers

Not everyone who joined the military suffered as much as privates—those in the lower ranks.

Officers, many of them college graduates, had much easier lives on military bases in the United States. At least 50 percent of all army officers were graduates of the college-based Reserve Officers Training Corps, or ROTC. In the air force 35 percent of the officers were ROTC graduates, and in the navy 20 percent of officers had served in ROTC.

ROTC cadets attended classes taught by military officers at college campuses across the country. In 1965 there were 165,000 cadets enrolled in the ROTC. As the war progressed, enrollment in college military programs fell drastically and by 1972 there were little more than fifty thousand students enrolled in the ROTC. By the late sixties the program had also become a target for antiwar protesters. ROTC students were harassed and ROTC buildings were sometimes burned on college campuses.

Infantry officers who earned their commissions through ROTC passed through Fort Benning, Georgia, and attended the Infantry Officer

Basic Course, which sarcastic officers referred to as Killer College. Alfred S. Bradford, who faced heavy combat in Vietnam, recalls his heady early days at Fort Benning in *Some Even Volunteered:*

> Even before we (ROTC officers) had gone to war, we imagined ourselves back, telling our own stories to an awe-stricken audience. After all, Vietnam was our generation's great adventure and we had volunteered for it; we wanted to go to war. Training, however, was not war—it seemed to be a game of Cowboys and Indians, but we couldn't take it seriously. The instructors try to get through to us with one bare statement: "Listen up, gentlemen, or you will die in Vietnam."[58]

Unlike privates, ROTC officers lived lives of relative comfort and ease. Their quarters resembled college dorm rooms, where they slept two to a room and were supplied with candy and soda machines in the hallways. As college graduates, ROTC officers were often mocked by others who had earned their commissions the hard way—by serving in war.

Once in Vietnam, all officers—whether they had served in ROTC or not—had much more serious problems. Officers who were perceived as ordering their troops to take unjustified risks could become victims of "fragging," the practice of killing an officer by throwing a hand grenade at him. Army private Pete Zastrow recalls: "We were in one place where we had two brigades, and one of the two commanders couldn't stay in his office because people kept opening his door and throwing grenades under his desk."[59] Fragging was yet another distinguishing feature of the low morale during the Vietnam War. By 1972

*Ohio State University students protest the ROTC on their campus in May 1970.*

an estimated fourteen hundred officers were killed by their own troops.

## The Mission

All military personnel were trained to follow orders and fight. They were also given classes about the nature of their mission and the cultural practices of their enemy. Many soldiers, especially early in the decade, had no knowledge of Vietnam or the Vietnamese. Mike McCain, a marine who served in Vietnam in 1967–68, recalls:

> I knew [Vietnam] was somewhere west of San Francisco. I knew vaguely where it was. I thought I was a fairly well informed young person. But looking back, there were . . . things I didn't know . . . [such as]

the international politics of what we were doing in Vietnam. . . . I had no knowledge of it at all.[60]

The anticommunist rhetoric of the 1950s and 1960s was particularly vehement, and many young people had learned at school rallies and in the national media that the dictator-run communist governments like those in the Soviet Union and Vietnam were the ultimate in human evil. John Niffin, who served in Vietnam in 1965, remembers: "I was brought up to believe that the communists were the Antichrist; you know—they were going to destroy western civilization. The worst thing in the world was a [communist]."[61] Soldiers were also taught about the Vietnamese people in extremely racist terms. They were called "subhuman" and referred to only by racial epithets.

*American soldiers were not well received by the South Vietnamese.*

Alfred S. Bradford faced heavy combat in Vietnam. In his book *Some Even Volunteered*, he writes of his first days back home:

"In forty-eight hours I went from a combat zone in Vietnam to my home in Appleton, Wisconsin. . . . My father wanted to [know] what did it all mean?

I said, 'It doesn't mean anything. The whole thing isn't worth one dead American.'

I had been awake for forty-eight hours. When I finally got to sleep, I dreamed I was in Vietnam. I saw three lieutenants, my friends, who had died there. 'We want to live,' they said to me.

I dreamt about them every night for a week. When I stopped dreaming about them, I felt as though I had betrayed and abandoned them. . . .

For days I stayed up late, slept fitfully, dreamed of the dead, woke early.

Then one night I heard a footstep on the back stair. NVA [North Vietnamese Army].

My heart pounded. But I was in my own bed in my own home. Perhaps I had dozed off, perhaps it was a dream . . . or had I heard a burglar? I was shaking, I moved as slowly as though I were in a dream . . . until I put my hand on the revolver in my desk. Immediately I was calm. I walked to the head of the stairs and flipped on the light. The stairs were empty.

'You fool,' I said to myself. 'You must have been dreaming.'

*But*, I replied, *it had sounded so real*.

'Relax. Go back to bed.'

*All right, but I'm not letting go of this revolver.*

*Am I going crazy?*

I waited. I had heard a footstep . . . or I was crazy . . . or the dead do rise (but we can't see them with the lights on).

*Was I going to be one of those veterans who goes out for a cup of [coffee], has a flashback, and wastes a café full of people?*"

## The War

After basic training many soldiers were shipped directly to Vietnam. By 1968 there were over 550,000 American soldiers "in country." Unlike the picture painted for the soldiers by army propaganda, most Vietnamese citizens were not happy to see the Americans and did not view them as liberators from communist aggression. Many civilians in South Vietnam supported the communist-backed North Vietnamese Army (NVA) either voluntarily or through threats and intimidation. In addition, the war was mostly fought in the south—over 4 million tons of American bombs were dropped on South Vietnam. By comparison, in World War II, the United States used about 2 million tons of bombs in Europe, Africa, the South Pacific, and Asia. South Vietnam was devastated. Roads, bridges, communications facilities, and industrial centers were destroyed. Agriculture practices were brought to a halt, oil reserves were destroyed, and cities were reduced to rubble. Fresh-faced young recruits who flew into this destruction were often appalled, as Farber writes:

For almost all the men, arrival in Vietnam was a shocking experience. Most men deplaned not to the sights and smells of war but to a seemingly chaotic, hustling world of poor Asian people . . . few of whom seemed to regard them as a liberating force. The men rode off to get their field assignments in buses with windows protected by wire mesh [to keep civilians from throwing hand grenades into the windows].[62]

NVA foot soldiers did not wear uniforms, and they had infiltrated almost every city and village where Americans were stationed. It was often impossible for American soldiers to identify the enemy among the civilians. Farber continues:

As a result, American soldiers often died not in firefights but in ones and twos, picked off by snipers, blown up by booby traps, emasculated by mines laid on paths villagers walked down every day. Identifying the sniper or saboteur or nighttime assassin among the blank-faced peasantry was beyond the capacity of most Americans. The situation was infuriating, maddening, and demoralizing.[63]

Of the 2 million soldiers who served in Vietnam, about 200,000 saw actual combat. The rest worked behind the lines, making sure combat troops were supplied with weapons, food, transportation, medical care, and other necessary items. Many of those who saw combat were permanently changed by the experience.

In addition to the problems of war, the social upheaval that was taking place in the United States was also affecting the military, and the army was experiencing unprecedented problems within its ranks. Mirroring civilian society, drug abuse, racial conflicts, and disrespect for authority had become rampant. McCain recalls his drug use in Vietnam:

My first introduction to drugs was in Vietnam. I started smoking reefers there, speed, barbituates [sic], because there were times on operations where you didn't want to go

to sleep so the corpsman would give us a thousand-tab[let] jar of . . . straight meth amphetamine.[64]

For these reasons, military desertions rose to unparalleled levels. More than twenty-five thousand soldiers—over 5 percent—went AWOL (absent without leave) in the late 1960s. At the peak of the problem, a soldier deserted his post every six minutes.

## Marching Home Again

When veterans were released from the army, they came home to a country that had changed dramatically. Race riots and antiwar protests had become common occurrences, drugs were everywhere, and high-profile assassinations seemed to follow one another in rapid succession. In addition, as the war became increasingly unpopular, returning GIs were sometimes treated badly by the general population.

In March 1968 it was revealed that hundreds of South Vietnamese women, children, and old men had been killed by American troops in the small Vietnamese village of My Lai. Dramatic pictures of dead children lying in ditches were published in newspapers and magazines across the globe. As a result, a small percentage of returning GIs, even those who had not seen combat, were referred to by some as "baby killers." Several others were spat upon in airports, restaurants, and train stations. Frederick H. Giese, who served in the navy during the war, writes about his experience at the San Francisco International Airport in *Homecoming* by Bob Greene:

My family and I were standing in line [in a cafeteria] when, out of the blue, this middle-aged lady walked up to me with a bowl of potato salad in her hand. She threw the salad smack in the middle of my chest and spat what salad she had in her mouth in my face. Then she proceeded to call me a "baby killer" "war monger" and a lot of other vile names. . . .

This "lady" was no hippie. I sort of get the feeling it has been easy to "blame" hippies for things like this because they were easily identifiable, and because they did dramatically, in many cases, communicate their opposition to the Vietnam war. But the verbal and physical abuse of returning Vietnam veterans took place in all levels of American society.[65]

Other GIs did not have such negative experiences. Some were treated to dinner or free drinks in bars. And while it has become a popular part of American culture that thousands of GIs were spat upon and mistreated, others who served in Vietnam dispute the stories. Michael A. Wertz, who served three tours of duty in Vietnam, writes:

At no time did I see anyone spit upon the uniformed soldier in any major airport. True, at times there may have been some mild forms of protest in progress, but these events were not aimed directly at individuals. This was, however, a time when everybody had a strong opinion on the pros and cons of the war, and any GI making a mistake of asking for an opinion would certainly have received one. . . .

The social structure of the times was so strong, however, that I am sure that any GI or hippie who actually desired a confrontation could have found one, but the image of GIs having to run a path of flying saliva is totally wrong. If I didn't see it in my three trips to and from Vietnam . . . then I doubt

like hell that there was anything more than an isolated incident or two.[66]

## Antiwar Veterans

Antiwar sentiment was rampant among civilians in the United States, but there was also a notable percentage of GIs who were opposed to the war. There were those who spoke out against the war while living in the United States, and those who protested while serving in Vietnam. Others joined antiwar organizations after they had finished their tours of duty.

Antiwar soldiers spread information about their beliefs in what were called underground newspapers. By the end of the 1960s, there were at least 145 such newspapers published by GIs. Some of the more radical papers urged soldiers to desert or even kill their commanding officers;

*Veterans protest American involvement in the Vietnam War.*

# Veterans Protest the War

In the mid-sixties, army veteran Jan Barry became an outspoken opponent of the Vietnam War. In *Winter Soldiers* by Richard Stacewicz, Barry describes his first antiwar rally on April 15, 1967, in New York City.

"One of the stories of the peace movement that still hasn't really been told was the diversity. It wasn't just this hippie image that has determined the legend. This demonstration that I'm seeing for the first time was full of families in their Sunday best and younger people. This was pre-hippie. People in 1967 still had straight, narrow ties. . . .

There were some young guys in parts of uniform, or suits and ties, and some women and children. I don't think there were more than a dozen Vietnam veterans and some family members; but behind them—which to me at the time was far more impressive— was like regimental [in] size, I think 2,000 guys, marching in military formation wearing Veterans for Peace hats.

When we proceeded out of the park and down through Fifth Avenue and through the various other streets, people were ready to lynch [us], howling and screaming and throwing things. First they see a little group of dignitaries, which apparently included Martin Luther King . . . and a couple of other people carrying an American flag. They're . . . taking all this abuse. Then, there's this little band of people carrying a sign, 'Vietnam Veterans Against the War.' You heard this sea change in the crowd. 'What is this? [Imitating voices in the crowd.] Is that for real? [Angry tone.] It can't even be for real. This has got to be a joke.' Then behind that, this group that clearly is veterans. 'What!' I mean, this isn't what they expected. 'Who are these people? If they're involved, I've got to rethink my opposition to all these people, hollering and screaming at them.' You literally could feel and hear a change in these sidewalk crowds."

others had provocative names such as *Counterattack*, which was published at Fort Dix, New Jersey. Soldiers often found these papers in antiwar coffeehouses that operated near military bases. At these off-base sanctuaries, soldiers could listen to rock music, meet sympathetic supporters, and learn information about the war. Army private Jack McCloskey talks about his role at a coffeehouse called the Pentagon located near the Oakland Army base:

This was a place where GIs could come in and we would talk to them about things like a KP [kitchen duty], guard duty, foxholes, [things] like that. Our goals were . . . basically to educate young men going to Vietnam. Our role was to humanize. People were trained

that the enemy you're fighting is lesser than you. One of our jobs in the coffeehouse was saying to them, "Hey, these are mothers, these are fathers, these are sons, these are daughters; this is who you're going to be shooting at. They're no different from you."[67]

While some opposed the war while serving on American army bases, some of the most adamant antiwar protesters were veterans who had already fought in Vietnam. At first these veterans were afraid to relate their often-grisly war experiences to people at antiwar marches. Others realized if they joined together and told of the horrors of war, their voices would give legitimacy to the antiwar movement. For that reason, a group of veterans created the Vietnam Veterans

Against the War (VVAW), which, according to Stacewicz, was "the first antiwar organization in American history consisting of veterans who were protesting against a war from which they had just returned."[68]

Many antiwar veterans grew long hair and adopted the counterculture lifestyle. Others wore their full-dress uniforms complete with medals won for bravery. Some made the rounds of television and radio shows speaking out against the war while others traveled to Washington, D.C., to lobby senators and congressional representatives.

The presence of the VVAW at demonstrations gave instant credibility to the antiwar movement, and the often-painful decisions by veterans to oppose the war provided a powerful argument against America's role in Vietnam. As its popularity grew, the organization attracted thousands of new members every year. McCloskey explains his reasons for joining the VVAW:

> [We] made promises to dead people. The only way we could justify the deaths of our buddies over there [in Vietnam] was by saying, "We've got to stop it." We've got to stop it. Stop the killing. Stop the killing. [Tearfully.] Here in San Francisco [at antiwar demonstrations], that was the chant I remember hearing the most, "Stop the killing, stop the killing, stop the killing."[69]

## Back to Civilian Life

While some veterans protested the war, a large majority simply took off their uniforms and went home to begin life anew. Many hadn't yet celebrated their twenty-fifth birthdays, but they had undergone experiences that few civilians could understand. And they had returned to a country that had changed radically in a few short years. Some were only beginning to experience war-related mental and physical problems that would haunt them for decades.

After the war, some vets were diagnosed with a condition known as post-traumatic stress disorder (PTSD). This syndrome causes its victims to experience a wide range of problems as they try to adjust to daily life after serving in combat. Sufferers of PTSD experience irritability, depression, a sense of guilt for having survived while others did not, and difficulties in relating to other people. Nightmares, flashbacks to battle scenes, and overreactions to sudden noises are also common. Because of PTSD, some Vietnam vets could not hold down jobs or maintain normal family life. In the 1980s, an estimated 30 percent of homeless people living on American streets were Vietnam vets. According to Stacewicz, "Perhaps as many as one-fourth of all Vietnam veterans, and more than half of the combat veterans, suffer from the syndrome."[70]

Vets also experienced problems caused by the use of the herbicide Agent Orange. Because this chemical instantly kills plants, U.S. policy makers sprayed it in great amounts over the jungles of Vietnam. The goal was to strip the leaves from the trees and expose where the enemy was hiding. Few U.S. military personnel who used the substance were aware that Agent Orange contains dioxin, one of the most toxic chemicals ever synthesized. Later, soldiers who had come into contact with Agent Orange experienced liver and other cancers, immune-deficiency diseases, persistent pain, and many other problems.

Only a small percentage of men and women who served in Vietnam, however, experienced problems from Agent Orange. A large majority of vets simply returned home and resumed their lives with few problems. Like almost all other people who lived through the 1960s, they accepted the changes in society, took the good with the bad, and lived the lives of average Americans citizens in the decades that followed.

# The Protesters

While millions of Americans struggled to fulfill their obligations to the American military, the war in Vietnam was opposed by hundreds of thousands of people both young and old. The first national protest against the war in Washington, D.C., in 1965 attracted about twenty thousand people. By the late sixties, similar demonstrations would attract more than a quarter million people. When the protests began in the mid-sixties, they were largely peaceful, but by the end of the decade many had turned into violent confrontations. Between the riots in the ghettos, the acid tests in Haight-Ashbury, and rowdy antiwar protests, some people felt that American society was collapsing into anarchy.

## The Free Speech Movement

Even before Johnson began to escalate the war in Vietnam in late 1964, students at the University of California at Berkeley were organizing mass protests. Students had been using campus facilities to organize rallies to aid African Americans in their battle for equal rights. These demonstrations were opposed by several major corporations that contributed financially to UC Berkeley. In September 1964, school administrators enacted a campus policy that forbid political activities and fund-raising on campus.

Police attempted to enforce the rule by arresting Jack Weinberg, a student fund-raiser

who was defying the ban. Weinberg was placed in an Oakland police car, which was quickly surrounded by two thousand student protesters. The demonstrators refused to let the car move for thirty-two hours until authorities agreed to negotiate a settlement to the problem. The debate over free speech on the Berkeley campus continued for several months.

Meanwhile, the Free Speech Movement, or FSM, attracted thousands of student sup-

*An angry restaurant owner smashes an egg in the face of a demonstrator at a sit-in.*

In 1960 few Americans had ever heard of the small Southeast Asian country of Vietnam, a nation that was slightly smaller than the state of California, with a population of around 40 million. The United States, however, had been involved politically and militarily in Vietnam since the end of World War II.

In the 1950s Vietnam was a divided country. The government of North Vietnam was backed by Communist China and the Soviet Union. The noncommunist Republic of Vietnam (RVN) in the south was supported by the United States. In 1960 it appeared that the communists from the North would soon overrun South Vietnam. In response, President Kennedy sent sixteen thousand American military advisers to South Vietnam, who were unable to stop the 300,000 North Vietnamese communist guerrillas who took control of parts of South Vietnam in 1963.

American citizens and their leaders were fearful that the communists would take over the entire region of Southeast Asia including Thailand, Cambodia, Laos, and elsewhere. Fear of losing all of Southeast Asia to the communists justified the war in Vietnam to a majority of people in the United States.

After Kennedy's assassination, President Johnson immediately stepped up the war. Johnson ordered bombing missions on North Vietnam on August 4, 1964. On February 15, 1965, the Vietcong attacked the U.S. Army barracks in Pleiku, South Vietnam, killing several American soldiers. The president used this attack to initiate Operation Rolling Thunder, a massive bombing of North Vietnam. On March 8, fifty thousand U.S. Marine combat ground forces landed in Da Nang, South Vietnam, ostensibly to protect the U.S. Air Force base there. By the end of the year, another 150,000 marines and army troops would be stationed in Da Nang. The Vietnam War was now fully under way.

---

porters, many of whom had similar backgrounds. While the Berkeley campus was about 20 percent Jewish and 15 percent Catholic, about a full one-third of the protesters were Jewish but only 6 percent were Catholic. The protesters were almost all white and a large majority were majoring in anthropology, philosophy, English, or history. Few of the protesters belonged to fraternities or sororities and even fewer majored in business administration.

On December 2, 1964, over fifteen hundred students walked into the administrative offices at Sproul Hall and held a sit-in to protest the ban on political activities. Best-selling folk singer Joan Baez attended the sit-in and sang Bob Dylan's protest anthem "The Times They Are A-Changin" and several other songs. There was a festive mood among the students, and some equated the tone to a homecoming football game.

In *The Free Speech Movement*, by David Lance Goines, student protester Tom Weller describes the activities inside Sproul Hall after it was taken over by students:

The floors of [the building] were divided up for various activities: first floor was for sleeping, second floor was wide open for anything anybody wanted to do, third floor was study hall and fourth floor was study and sleeping area. Every floor had monitors in proportion to the number of people, and members of the [FSM] Steering Committee made themselves highly visible, talking with people and entering into impromptu discussions. After two movies . . . [Jewish holiday] Chanukah services, dancing and speeches, people settled down for the night, either to sleep or to study. [Two students] played a giant game of chess on linoleum-tile squares, using coke bottles for pawns and playing cards for the other pieces. Informal classes were held in corners and under stairwells. . . .[71]

Police moved in at about 5 A.M. on December 3 and started to arrest protesters. Students went limp to make it more difficult for police to move them, and many were simply dragged and bounced down the stairs of Sproul Hall. Nearly eight hundred students were eventually arrested, making it the largest mass arrest in California history at that time. As police arrested and detained the protesters, other students who had not been arrested climbed up ropes into the building's second-story windows to take their turn at being arrested and to create more work for authorities. It took police more than thirteen hours to clear the protesters out of the building.

## From Free Speech to Antiwar

The sit-in at Sproul Hall was the first of hundreds of student takeovers that would bring chaos to America's college campuses during the next eight years. Although the Berkeley protest had ended peacefully, police in later years would not be as gentle with demonstrators. As the war in Vietnam escalated, so too did the antiprotester tactics of authorities. Tear gas and rifles would become almost as commonplace on campuses as textbooks and blackboards.

The Berkeley protests made national headlines and quickly attracted thousands of young adults to Berkeley. Rubin explains the result:

The Free Speech Movement invited young kids to come to Berkeley for the action. So

thousands of refugees from New York and the Midwest flocked to live on the streets of Berkeley.

It was an easy life. The weather was warm and the seasons hardly changed. . . . You could always get by selling dope. Or you could hawk the [underground newspaper the Berkeley] *Barb* on weekends and make enough money for the rest of the week. There were always some guilty professors to panhandle. And some people started handicraft industries—sold jewelry, candles and other things they made—right on the Avenue.

Dig the straight student who came out of a Los Angeles suburb to get an education at Berkeley. Heading for his dormitory or apartment after a hard day at school, he passed down Telegraph Avenue: like walking through the revolution on the way home.[72]

The Free Speech Movement was about to disband in early March 1965 after having won the right to organize protests on campus. President Johnson, however, ordered fifty thousand U.S. Marine combat ground forces to South Vietnam at that time, and another hundred thousand would ship out before the end of the year. The FSM quickly transformed itself into the Vietnam's Day Committee, or VDC. Rubin explains the mission of the VDC:

We were putting out a weekly newspaper, organizing door-to-door discussions about Vietnam in the black ghetto in Oakland, sending out speakers everywhere, leafletting soldiers at airports telling them to desert, advising kids how to beat the draft, and coordinating research, petition drives, massive and mini-demonstrations. No government official could come to the Bay

Area without being haunted by a VDC reception team of psychic terrorists. . . . In one room crazies planned to rent planes and fly over the Rose Bowl dropping antiwar leaflets on the crowd. In another room crazier people planned a direct assault on the Oakland Army Terminal.[73]

While the VDC conducted demonstrations in Berkeley, a political group called Students for a Democratic Society, or SDS, organized students on hundreds of other campuses across the country. SDS put together the first major antiwar protests in Washington, D.C., on April 17, 1965. At that rally, twenty thousand people demonstrated against the government's policy in Vietnam. Five weeks later, on May 21 in Berkeley, over fifteen thousand students attended a rally to protest the war. Many of them carried signs with a new slogan: "MAKE LOVE NOT WAR."

## Escalating Violence

By 1967 over 500,000 Americans were stationed in Vietnam. During that year, 9,353 were killed and almost 100,000 wounded. As the war continued to grow so did the antiwar demonstrations. In the spring of 1967, a new group called the National Mobilization Committee to End the War in Vietnam, or MOBE, organized rallies across the country. In New York City almost 400,000 marched against the war; in San Francisco about fifty thousand came to protest. At both rallies, people carried banners and chanted popular slogans such as "Hell No, We Won't Go!" and

*Americans participate in a five-mile march in San Francisco in 1967 to protest the Vietnam War.*

"Hey, Hey, LBJ, How Many Kids Did You Kill Today!"[74]

These demonstrations were attended by a wide cross section of Americans, including long-haired hippies, short-haired office workers, well-dressed professionals, mothers pushing baby carriages, members of women's organizations, and black groups such as the Afro-Americans Against the War in Vietnam.

While protesters believed that they were simply exercising their rights to free speech guaranteed in the U.S. Constitution, tensions continued to grow between authorities and demonstrators. This was clearly shown during protests at the Oakland Induction Center. The Induction Center was the main West Coast shipping point of draftees, fresh from basic training, who were on their way to Vietnam. Protesters believed that if they could prevent soldiers from entering or leaving the building, they would make a powerful statement.

When about eight thousand protesters attempted to close down the Oakland Induction Center in October 1967, they were met by two thousand riot police. By this time, street actions had become almost monthly events in Berkeley and Oakland, and authorities were ready to use violence as a means of discouraging further

## The Influence of Television

As with many other events in the 1960s, television greatly influenced public opinion about the Vietnam War. In 1968 Vietcong guerrillas launched a surprise attack on almost every U.S. stronghold in South Vietnam. Known as the Tet Offensive, this was one of the most heated and drawn-out battles of the war. Over the course of several months, the United States dropped over 220 million tons of bombs on Vietnam. In *The Movement and the Sixties*, Terry Anderson writes about news images generated during the Tet Offensive, and their influence on Americans at home:

"Tet produced sensational scenes, and they flashed across America in newspapers and on television: U.S. officials defending themselves, shooting out of embassy windows. Marines in [the city of] Hue . . . ducking for cover, firing at the enemy hiding behind scarred, ancient walls. American planes strafing villages, dropping napalm canisters that burst into rolling fireballs. A U.S. Army officer standing on the outskirts of what remained of a Mekong Delta village stating, 'We had to destroy [the village], in order to save it.' The haggard faces, the haunted eyes of [American] defenders at Khe Sanh. The South Vietnam national police chief walking down the street with a ragged Vietcong suspect, stopping in front of reporters, nonchalantly lifting his pistol, pointing it at the man's temple—pulling the trigger.

[Television cameras] zoomed in and showed helicopters machine-gunning peasants running below in rice paddies. 'If he's running,' said a helicopter crewman, 'he must be a Vietcong.' These scenes, these statements, became symbolic for the war. Many Americans wondered whether all the brutality would bring victory, or whether it was just pointless. Editors of *Christian Century* wrote: 'This is the genius of our war effort—to destroy Vietnam in order to save it.' The twisted, tragic face of war confronted American viewers, and news anchormen began to warn viewers: 'The following scenes might not be suitable viewing for children.' Indeed, most citizens realized in 1968 that war really was hell."

protest. Television camera operator V. T. Ronay describes the situation in Oakland on October 17, 1967:

> The police completely sealed off the streets leading to the center. There was no possibility of regrouping and coming down other streets. The image is of canyons between buildings with bulldozers clearing away the impediments to the proceedings. As a machine mashes what it does not move so the people crouching in the doorways were not permitted to leave and were trapped and beaten and when eventually given room to rise and run, they were chased and hit by swinging clubs. . . .

> The first and most striking shock in the events was the disparity of size between the police and the demonstrators, mainly kids. I had never noticed how small and skinny students . . . are. . . . [T]he people have only their skulls and their screams. The line of offense had the helmets, muscles, gloves and a dedication to violence. . . . I have always viewed billy clubs as instruments of pushing and poking—not in the prehistoric sense of a deadly weapon used to break bones, damage kidneys and ovaries and crush skin.[75]

During the three-hour street battle with Oakland police, protesters threw up barricades using cars, bus benches, newspaper racks, garbage cans, and potted trees to keep the police at bay. Tear gas filled the air as demonstrators blocked intersections and prevented buses full of inductees from arriving at the center. The demonstration eventually ended as night fell, but about twenty blocks of Oakland were left littered with debris and spray-painted with antiwar slogans.

The police were not the only people opposing protesters. A backlash grew against the

*Vietnam War protesters square off with police at a demonstration in Oakland, California.*

demonstrations, and working-class Americans such as construction workers and World War II veterans could also be seen at antiwar rallies yelling at the hippies to cut their hair. These pro-war demonstrators carried signs that proclaimed "USA LOVE IT OR LEAVE IT!"[76] At every major demonstration in New York City, marchers had eggs thrown at them and faced verbal and physical abuse. Those who opposed the war were often labeled traitors and communists and some even had red paint thrown on them.

Those who controlled the media generally supported the war, and publishers of magazines and newspapers actively encouraged rough treatment of antiwar protesters, as Anderson explains:

> The press ridiculed demonstrators. *Life* called protesters "chronic showoffs" who

failed to realize that the war was "a last stand for democracy or freedom or even that the destiny of the U.S. is at stake." The *Chicago Tribune* called on the government to "act in the toughest way possible," and the *New York Daily News* demanded that the "Communist-incited beatniks, pacifists and damned idiots" be tried for treason. The *Dallas Morning News* scoffed at the "transparent motives" of the "kooks and Communists," and from Mississippi, the *Jackson Daily News* had a suggestion for demonstrators: "This is the time for police brutality if there ever was one."[77]

## Protesting the Draft

Most of the people at the antiwar demonstrations were opposed to the Vietnam War on moral and philosophical grounds. They did not believe that the United States should be meddling in the affairs of a foreign country when there was so much work to be done at home regarding racism, poverty, and injustice. Many of the men in the crowd, however, had more personal reasons for opposing the war. In a historical coincidence, just as the first wave of baby boomers were reaching their eighteenth birthdays, the U.S. government began to drastically increase the amount of young men drafted into military service.

All men between the ages of eighteen and twenty-six were required to register for the draft, and in 1964, 1.7 million men—the first wave of baby boomers—reached the age of eighteen. In April 1965 the Selective Service sent out 13,700 draft notices. In May the number of draft notices reached 15,100. And by July it had climbed to 27,400. In December over 40,000 men were ordered to take their army physical and join the U.S. military.

Previous to the escalation of the war, the Selective Service granted a wide range of deferment that allowed men to avoid military service. About two-thirds of draft-age men were exempt from serving because they worked in agriculture, went to college, had children, or were conscientious objectors—religiously or morally opposed to all war.

A majority of young men avoided the draft because they were college students. As a result, many white middle-class men from the suburbs were able to stay out of the army. A large percentage of those drafted were poor, rural residents, or black men who were denied access to college because of racial discrimination. As such, 24 percent of those killed in Vietnam in 1965 were African Americans. When confronted with this fact, in later years the military somewhat reduced the combat role of blacks to lower the casualty rates.

David Harris was married to folk singer Joan Baez in the sixties and spent twenty months in a federal prison because of his refusal to be inducted into the army. In *Our War* he explains how deferments shaped the army:

> [Those who were drafted were] mostly the boys of the poor, the sons of the social edge, the less than fortunate, the oddballs who fell through a crack, those who couldn't afford to go to school full-time, those who worked with their hands or their backs, the lost, the lazy, the penitent, the undercapitalized, the unwanted . . . [and] the needy. . . .[78]

## Dodging the Draft

As the war escalated, more middle-class men found themselves receiving draft notices. As a result, resistance to the draft increased and hundreds of protests and sit-ins focused on local government buildings where draft boards convened. The demonstrations usually featured men burning their draft cards—thick paper documents resembling driver's licenses, which stated their Selective Service classifications. Men were required by law to carry these cards with them at all times, and, as such, card burning became a common form of protest. Congress enacted laws making the offense punishable by a $10,000 fine and a five-year prison term. This law also authorized the FBI and other law enforcement agencies to conduct surveillance upon those who burned their cards or incited others to do so.

William Sloane Coffin, antiwar activist and chaplain at Yale University, remembers counseling students who wanted to mail their draft cards back to the draft boards:

I was spending an awful lot of time with students who were in considerable agony

as to whether or not to turn in their draft cards, and what it would do to jeopardize their futures. These were very real dilemmas, you know. If someone wanted to be a doctor, for example, he would jeopardize the chances of getting any federal funding for his studies. Without that you can't become a doctor, unless you're exceedingly rich. . . . Those kinds of problems were very real, and I spent many, many hours on them. By turning in draft cards as a protest against the war, students and resisters were opening themselves up for a total of five years [in prison] or ten thousand dollars in fines. It was a very courageous act.[79]

Most men did not burn their draft cards or return them to the government. Instead, they considered dozens of ways to "dodge" the draft. As a result, enrollment into community colleges, colleges, and universities soared during

*Young men burn their draft cards on the steps of the Pentagon.*

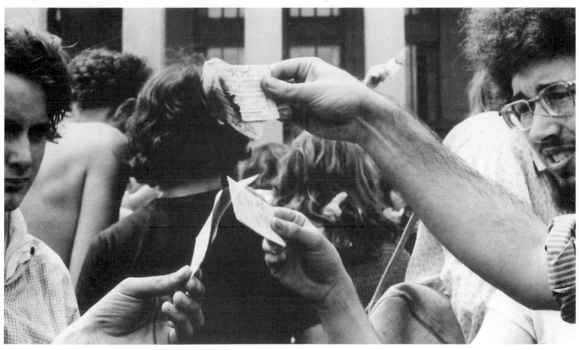

the war. Those who were called in for their pre-induction physicals tried to convince their local draft boards that they were not fit to serve. Many antiwar groups employed counselors who instructed potential draftees on ways to avoid service, as Farber writes:

> Through friendly doctors and psychiatrists they received medical and psychological deferments. Some half a million young men, mainly in earnest, became conscientious objectors to the war and then did alternative national service. . . . Young men learned from the rapidly expanding core of "draft counselors" to fake symptoms at their pre-induction exams, to claim to be gay, to claim

to be a member of a subversive organization, to be disruptive, and so on.[80]

Some men who feared military service in Vietnam took drastic actions in order to be disqualified from the military on physical grounds. They took massive amounts of drugs or stayed awake for days before appearing for their draft physicals. According to Dougan and Lipsman,

> Some jabbed pins into their arms to simulate the "tracks" made by heroin addicts or artificially raised their blood pressure with caffeine and other drugs. Others aggravated sports injuries such as bad knees or, like one University of Michigan student who ate

*Columbia University students stage a sit-in April 1968, in New York City.*

three large pizzas every night for six months, made sure that they exceeded the military weight limit for their height.[81]

Other draft dodgers went into hiding in Canada. By 1969 over a hundred thousand American men of draft age had run away to Canada or other countries.

## Student Takeover at Columbia

Many felt that the most effective way to avoid the draft was to oppose the war as loudly as possible, and by 1968 student protests were making daily news across America. In addition to resisting the war, young people also rallied against university-based weapons research, discrimination against blacks, and other issues. According to Farber, "Many of the most radical students, often associated with SDS, believed that in order to 'bring the war home' they should take advantage of any possible political issue to disrupt 'business as usual' on their campuses. This plan resulted in a number of spectacularly confrontational protests."[82]

One of the more notable campus protests occurred on the Columbia University campus. Students were outraged over Columbia's membership in the Institute of Defense Analysis (IDA), an association of a dozen universities that advised the Department of Defense in matters of science, engineering, and other fields. After a short protest rally on April 23, 1968, more than seven hundred students took over Low Library, the administrative offices at Hamilton Hall, and other buildings on campus. The student occupation lasted more than six days and attracted wide coverage from the national and international news media.

Although the campus takeover was one of the most widely covered events of the sixties, it was a spontaneous one in which Hamilton Hall was seized and a momentum built to take over

other buildings. The demonstration took on a festive air, and even students who were not involved in the SDS or other political organizations joined in the protest. Nancy Biberman, one of the members of the SDS who participated in the Columbia takeover, describes the events:

It was a counterculture event, as well as a political action. There were elaborate feasts in some buildings, socializing, music, dancing. There was a wedding in [the] Fayerwethyer [building] and two people who were married called themselves Andrea and Richard Fayerwethyer. In Low Library, there was this guy who was sort of a literary type on campus, not an activist. And the events just sort of captured his imagination. Someone took pictures of him sitting in the president's lavish mahogany office, smoking his cigars, his feet up on the desk. He was a real character: long black hair, long black mustache, an arty type. It was a great picture. And it *enraged* the university. This was the ultimate degradation, this dirty character sitting in the president's chair.[83]

The photos of the student in the president's office was printed on the front pages of newspapers across the globe and came to symbolize student protest for years to come.

## "Kicks, Punches, and Billy Clubs"

The strike lasted for days and during this time students held meetings, talked about issues, read newspaper and magazine stories about the occupation, and drew up long lists of demands, which were debated for hours on end. Biberman describes her feelings during the occupation:

It's hard to describe, but there was an incredible exhilaration, that here we were making history, changing the world. We had done something that nobody else had done before, and, who knows, maybe we were going to *make the revolution* at Columbia. This was the beginning of the end [for straight America]. Everybody believed that the universe would never be the same, that society would be irrevocably changed, that there'd be a revolution in [the] United States within five years, and a whole new social order. This is really what people believed, and I did, too. It was that kind of heady experience, it really was.[84]

Negotiations with campus administrators dragged on for days while hundreds of police surrounded the school. Finally, after six days the police acted to evict the protesters at 2:30 A.M. When it was over, 722 were arrested and 148 were injured, including 20 policemen. Charles Kaiser describes the scene:

Long-haired students taunted helmeted policemen with verbal abuse and sometimes threw rocks, bottles, and chairs; they themselves were subdued with kicks, punches, and billy clubs. Many students were clearly eager for a fight, but the police were far more experienced with violence than they were, and it showed. . . . Some of the students inside Avery and Mathematics halls were dragged facedown over marble steps leading to police vans waiting on Amsterdam Avenue. In other parts of the campus, away from the occupied buildings, platoons of police assaulted students wherever they found them. Outside the college gates on Broadway, mounted policemen . . . charged anyone who looked as if he might be a demonstrator.[85]

While the actions at Columbia were generating headlines, April 26 was also a day that the National Mobilization Committee had called for a general strike in which students were asked to stay away from school to protest the war. Without any violence or bloodshed, over a million high school and college students boycotted school for that one day. Not only was it the largest student walkout in American history, but the boycott became an international event with student strikes also held in Mexico City, Paris, Tokyo, and Prague.

The next day in New York City, a hundred thousand antiwar protesters marched down Fifth Avenue to Central Park. They heard speeches by New York mayor John Lindsay, African American comedian and activist Dick Gregory, and Coretta Scott King, widow of Martin Luther King Jr. Folk musicians Pete Seeger and Arlo Guthrie entertained the crowd. Meanwhile, twenty-five thousand prowar demonstrators marched in the Loyalty Day Parade only several blocks away.

## Days of Rage in Chicago

The spring violence at Columbia clearly demonstrated the direction in which the country was moving. By the time the Democrats were ready to hold their presidential convention in Chicago in August 1968, the United States had become a violently polarized nation. While only a small percentage of Americans supported the tactics of the antiwar protesters, 56 percent now said they no longer supported the war in Vietnam. As the Democrats made plans to elect Hubert Humphrey as their presidential candidate, a new political group known as the Youth International Party, or Yippies, made plans to disrupt the Chicago events.

The Yippies, founded by Abbie Hoffman and Jerry Rubin, advocated outrageous actions to attract media attention to their cause. By spreading the word in antiwar underground newspapers, Yippie quickly became a national buzzword and tens of thousands of protesters were notified of their plans to hold a demonstration in Chicago. The Yippies planned an event during the convention called the Festival of Life. Their chief publicity stunt was to run a pig, named Pigasus, for president. Hoffman documents other outrageous plans Yippies made for the week:

> We would secure a large park, sponsor workshops, exhibits, demonstrations and rock concerts in contrast to the deadly doldrums that would go on inside Convention Hall. True, there would be . . . high jinks, but our strategy did not include plans for organized violence or riot although our fanciful literature carried our dope-induced hallucinations. We revealed that the Potheads' Benevolent Association had been busy all spring strewing [marijuana] seeds in the vacant lots of Chicago, anticipating the ideal growing weather of the predicted Long Hot Summer. We spread the rumor that battalions of super-potent yippie males were getting in shape to seduce female convention-goers and that yippie agents were posing as hookers. There was no end to our nefarious plans. We would dress up people like Viet Cong and send them into the streets to shake hands like ordinary American politicians. We would paint cars taxi-yellow, pick up delegates and drop them in Wisconsin.[86]

Police responded to these taunts by bringing together one of the largest antiprotest forces ever assembled in the United States. There were 11,000 Chicago police; 6,000 National Guardsmen with M-1 rifles, shotguns, and gas canisters; and 7,500 fully-armed U.S.

Army troops. In addition, the government sent over 1,000 federal agents from the FBI, CIA, and military intelligence units. They conducted wiretapping and electronic eavesdropping against the protesters and news media.

The humorous intent of the protest spelled out in the Yippie flier quickly turned serious during the convention. On August 28, the last night of the convention, around five thousand demonstrators assembled to protest. When they marched to the convention center where the Democrats were nominating Humphrey, their progress was halted by police lines. Those at the back began to push, and those in the front sat down in the streets. Peaceful arrests ensued, but around 8 P.M., someone threw something at one of the officers. This set off a melee, which Anderson describes:

> Boom! The police exploded into the crowd. Shouts, confusion, panic. Gas canisters exploding. Police clubbing. People screaming, bleeding. Some ran down streets, into hotel lobbies, back to the park. More cops arrived. Patrol wagons appeared. Tear gas floated into the Hilton, up the air vents, and into the suite of the vice president, who was preparing his acceptance speech. On the streets, chanting . . . "The Whole World is Watching."[87]

Police beat protesters, news reporters, and doctors and nurses who attempted to help the wounded. Inexplicably, police charged a group of middle-aged delegates and pushed them through the plate-glass windows of the hotel restaurant.

## Issues of War and Peace

By the end of the decade, some students had become violently radicalized by the protests and were intent on fomenting revolution and destroying the U.S. government. Groups such as the Weathermen planted bombs under police cars and attempted to blow up research labs at universities.

Protests against the war continued until the United States finally pulled all of its military forces out of Vietnam in 1973. When the war ended, student protest organizations quickly disbanded. By the mid-1970s, there was little

friction on college campuses as the U.S. economy entered a long recession. With skyrocketing inflation and tens of thousands of workers losing their jobs, Vietnam seemed a distant memory to many.

Long after the guns fell silent and the shouting died down, Americans continued to debate the war in Vietnam and the protest it aroused. While some believed that the protesters aided the North Vietnamese by giving them moral

*Chicago police arrest a demonstrator in Grant Park during a riot outside the 1968 Democratic National Convention.*

# Unrestrained Police Violence

After the riots at the Democratic Convention in Chicago in 1968, President Johnson appointed lawyer Daniel Walker to chair the National Commission on the Causes and Prevention of Violence to examine the causes of the melee. The report was released in December 1968 after the commission reviewed over 20,000 pages of statements from 3,437 eyewitnesses and participants, 180 hours of film, and over 12,000 still photographs. The summary was printed on the Chicago 1968 Democratic National Convention: Bibliography website.

"During the week of the Democratic National Convention, the Chicago police were the targets of mounting provocation by both word and act. It took the form of obscene epithets, and of rocks, sticks, bathroom tiles, and even human feces hurled at police by demonstrators. Some of these acts had been planned; others were spontaneous or were themselves provoked by police action. Furthermore, the police had been put on edge by widely published threats of attempts to disrupt both the city and the Convention.

That was the nature of the provocation. The nature of the response was unrestrained and indiscriminate police violence on many occasions, particularly at night.

That violence was made all the more shocking by the fact that it was often inflicted upon persons who had broken no law, disobeyed no order, made no threat. These included peaceful demonstrators, onlookers, and large numbers of residents who were simply passing through, or happened to live in, the areas where confrontations were occurring.

Newsmen and photographers were singled out for assault, and their equipment deliberately damaged. Fundamental police training was ignored; and officers, when on the scene, were often unable to control their men. As one police officer put it: 'What happened didn't have anything to do with police work.'"

---

support, others pointed out that the Vietnamese were ready to fight for years in order to drive the United States from their soil. At the same time, the antiwar activists exposed hundreds of incidents where the U.S. government had lied to the people it was sworn to represent about how, where, and why the war had been waged.

While those issues were debated, one point remained clear: The decade of the 1960s was one of the few times in American history when hundreds of thousands of Americans engaged in long-running verbal and physical battles against one another and their government over issues of war and peace.

# The Changing Roles of Women

The 1960s was a decade when, inspired by African Americans' protests, almost every other American minority group began to demand equal rights. Native Americans, Hispanics, homosexuals, and others believed that they too should be guaranteed equal rights in housing, employment, and other areas. While women made up the majority in the United States, they continued to face gender discrimination through most of the decade. Although the counterculture was trying to change the world, attitudes toward women had changed little since the 1950s.

A large majority of American women in the 1960s were mothers and housewives. Many were active volunteers at churches, schools, the PTA, Girl Scouts, and various charities. In business and politics, however, women continued to find themselves in a world controlled almost exclusively by men. With a few notable exceptions, only a tiny percentage of women were doctors, lawyers, politicians, or corporate executives.

## The Status of Women

In 1963 President Kennedy created the Commission on the Status of Women to study issues facing women. The commission, chaired by Eleanor Roosevelt, wife of former president Franklin Roosevelt, issued a report stating that women faced discrimination in many ways. June Sochen sums up the commission's findings in *Herstory:*

The professions did not admit [women], the graduate schools did not encourage them, and indeed even elementary schools discouraged girls from seeking advanced education, programming them early on to accept their cultural role. The Commission recommended a number of specific actions to remedy the situation:

More flexible admission requirements on the part of the colleges.

Government-sponsored day-care centers.

Adequate job-counseling services for women.

An end to discrimination in hiring and employment practices within the federal government.[88]

Kennedy supported the commission's findings, and the same year the report was issued, the president signed the Equal Pay Act, which established equal pay for men and women performing the same job duties. After Kennedy's death, Congress passed the Civil Rights Act. Title VII of the act bars employment discrimination on the basis of race, sex, and other grounds. The bill also established the Equal Employment Opportunity Commission (EEOC), which received over fifty thousand complaints of gender discrimination before 1970. Just as African Americans had discovered, however, the passage of bills such as the Civil Rights Act did little to change ingrained attitudes in society, women's rights activists realized it would take years of protest and lawsuits to transform American culture.

## Women's Roles in Society

In the years before the women's liberation movement, women were expected to perform the duties of stay-at-home mothers and societal pressures insured strict roles for both genders. It was widely accepted that men were supposed to be tough, individualistic, unemotional, solid, and aggressive. A woman's basic need, it was said, was to be a wife, mother, and homemaker. Her primary achievement and fulfillment was child bearing.

While some women were disenchanted by society's rules, the concept of feminism as it is known today did not exist. As Farber writes, the conventional wisdom stated that

[men] should control political and economic life and . . . women should participate in these public spheres, if at all, as men's subordinates. . . . [M]en had the right to head their households and . . . women should serve them as help-mates responsible for housekeeping and day-to-day child rearing; and finally . . . women were best measured by their beauty, charm, and sexual restraint and men by their accomplishments, power, and sexual prowess.[89]

*President Kennedy meets with appointees to discuss the status of women in America.*

Traditional beliefs about women began to change in 1963 when Betty Friedan, a suburban mother of three and a freelance writer, published *The Feminine Mystique*. Friedan was inspired to write the book after she attended the fifteenth reunion of Smith College's class of 1942. Friedan conducted a survey of her classmates and discovered that in spite of their education and overall prosperous lives, many women were extremely unhappy because of their limited roles in society. The women in Friedan's book, according to Sochen, said that

their superior education had promised them intellectual excitement and full use of their mental abilities. Instead, they married, had children, and for hours each day were utterly bored by busywork. Mrs. Friedan blamed advertisers, women's magazine editors, and . . . the culture for

*Betty Friedan, author of* The Feminine Mystique, *suggested that women were bored with the traditional roles society imposed on them.*

The opening pages of *The Feminine Mystique*, published by Betty Friedan in 1963, express the dissatisfaction women felt in the early sixties:

"The problem lay buried, unspoken, for many years in the minds of American women. It was a strange stirring, a sense of dissatisfaction, a yearning that women suffered in the middle of the twentieth century in the United States. Each suburban wife struggled with it alone. As she made the beds, shopped for groceries, matched slipcover material, ate peanut butter sandwiches with her children, chauffeured Cub Scouts and Brownies, lay beside her husband at night—she was afraid to ask even of herself the silent question—"Is this all?"

For over fifteen years there was no word of this yearning in the millions of words written about women, for women, in all the columns, books, and articles by experts telling women their role was to seek fulfillment as wives and mothers. Over and over women heard in voices of tradition . . . that they could desire no greater destiny than to glory in their own femininity. Experts told them how to catch a man and keep him, how to breastfeed children and handle their toilet training . . . how to buy a dishwasher, bake bread, cook gourmet snails, and build a swimming pool with their own hands; how to dress, look, and act more feminine and make marriage more exciting; how to keep . . . their sons from growing into delinquents. They were taught to pity the neurotic, unfeminine, unhappy women who wanted to be poets or physicists or presidents. They learned that truly feminine women do not want careers, higher education, political rights—the independence and the opportunities that the old-fashioned feminists fought for."

women's unhappiness. Women had been promised that marriage and the products of affluence would compose a good life—they discovered otherwise. The image of women as buyers and consumers satisfied [producers of advertisements] and manufacturers but not American women. In essence, Betty Friedan's solution to the woman's dilemma was to find stimulating, personally rewarding work outside the home—either a career that could be interrupted for child-bearing or an interesting part-time job.[90]

*The Feminine Mystique* became an instant best-seller and inspired thousands of women to pursue their own careers. Gender discrimination, however, remained widespread throughout the sixties, and women who wanted to become professionals faced many hurdles in the workforce.

## Single Women

The stereotypes of women as mothers and housewives began to change considerably in the mid-1960s. While Betty Friedan recommended that women continue to marry—but later in life—television, movies, and magazines were promoting the image of the happy-go-lucky single girl with a flip hairstyle, polka-dot stockings, long false eyelashes, and a miniskirt.

*Helen Gurley Brown's book,* Sex and the Single Girl, *presented a new image of the 1960s woman.*

The idealized concept of the "perky" unmarried woman became fashionable in the early sixties after the publication of the groundbreaking book *Sex and the Single Girl* by Helen Gurley Brown in 1962. Brown opened the book with these words:

> Far from being a creature to be pitied and patronized, the single girl is emerging as the newest glamour girl of our times. . . . [W]hen a man thinks of a married woman, no matter how lovely she is, he must inevitably picture her . . . fixing little children's lunches, or scrubbing them down because they've fallen in a mudhole. . . . When a man thinks of a single woman, he pictures her alone in her apartment, smoothe legs sheathed in pink

silk Capri pants, lying tantalizingly among dozens of satin cushions, trying to read but not very successfully, for HE is in the room—filling her thoughts, her dreams, her life.[91]

*Sex and the Single Girl* quickly became a worldwide best-seller published in twenty-three countries. It was also made into a movie starring Natalie Wood. The book became, according to the Sterns, "the first sixties manifesto for women in general, perky girls in particular."[92]

After the success of her book, Brown was appointed editor of *Cosmopolitan* magazine. The magazine, simply known as *Cosmo*, was full of tips, formulas, tricks, and tests to help single women, or "Cosmo Girls," in the world of dating, decorating, and entertaining. Along with shallow articles with names such as "The Man-Trap Apartment,"[93] *Cosmo* also published well-written features by women authors such as Nora Ephron, Gael Greene, and others. And unlike other magazines at the time that were written for general audiences, *Cosmo* was the first to focus on a well-defined segment of the population—the single working woman. As a result, readership soared and Brown became the spokesperson for the swinging sixties single woman.

## College Life and the Pill

While single working women were free to pursue their lives in relative freedom, many single young women were in college. As protests erupted on college campuses over free speech and the war in Vietnam, many women continued to be limited by school regulations that strictly controlled their behavior. As Farber explains:

> Given the prevailing wisdom of the early 1960s, which placed sexual responsibility al-

most completely on women . . . [these rules] almost always prescribed women's behavior and not men's. The University of Michigan student handbook in 1962, for example, devoted nine of its fifteen pages to curfews and [violation] penalties for women. Men had no such limits or penalties. At the University of Kansas in 1965, a woman wrote in the second SDS campus newsletter: "Women . . . are regulated in the most minute aspects of everyday existence. . . ."

Equal rights to come home late from a date sounds frivolous. But young women fighting for that right often came to see other rules and social practices that discriminated against women. And many a young woman began to ponder why various authorities (usually men) had the right to control her own life and sexuality.[94]

The rules that governed college coeds were written at a time when young women were away from home for the first time and authorities feared these women might become pregnant before marriage. By the mid-sixties, that fear had been all but eliminated by the birth control pill, which prevented pregnancy.

"The Pill," as it was called, was a major factor in changing the lives of sixties women whether single or married. Invented in the 1950s, the birth control pill was approved by the U.S. Food and Drug Administration in 1960. Within eighteen months over half a million women were on the pill, and by 1964 that number had jumped to 3.5 million. In 1966

## *Cosmo*'s Decorating Tips

*Cosmopolitan* was the most popular women's magazine in the 1960s. Millions of women followed the magazine's advice in matters of diet, fashion, and even home decorating. In *Sixties People*, Jane and Michael Stern list decorating tips for single women as reported in *Cosmo*.

"A perky apartment was as harebrained and fun-loving as a girl's budget allowed. It was assumed that the reader was squeaking by on a tiny salary, so most suggestions emphasized cleverness over cost. Ferns hung from macramé holders knotted to look like big-eyed owls. Bathtubs and toilet-seat covers were festooned with Rickie Tickie Stickies—glue-backed [plastic] daisies that made boring old bathroom fixtures come alive. Fun rugs . . . helped cover over the sad linoleum floor, and a lemon-scented freshener gave the air a happy citrus tang.

The perky girl's palate for home decoration was shades of screaming citrus. The prime color was yellow, the brightest possible yellow of lemons and sunshine. . . . Wow-tones such as tropical orange and stinging pink were feminine and helped give the perky girl's digs a jolt of eccentricity in contrast to contemporary split-level family homes. . . .

[For furniture, she] chose vinyl chair-shaped bean bags as squishy as a down pillow or inflatable rubber couches that got blown up with a bicycle pump. Or just pillows . . . nothing but pillows! . . .

The best way to make an apartment truly perky was to do it all yourself. Creativity was an esteemed quality in the sixties; it was evidence of a fresh eye and a love of novelty, both of which proved one modern. Making something cute from nothing was one of the fundamental perky-curl of talents."

over 50 percent of all married women under the age of twenty, and 81 percent of college graduates under the age of twenty-five, were taking birth control pills. In *The Century of Sex*, James R. Peterson explains why the pill was so popular:

> Women took the Pill to postpone their first pregnancies, to avoid falling into the family trap as described by Friedan in *The Feminine Mystique*. Their parents may have had the perfect family—four children one after another—but that model shackled a woman to one role. Wives of the sixties used the Pill to space the births of their children, to create time to complete degrees or advance careers. The Pill granted the means to achieve the original feminist vision. Single women used the Pill to postpone their first marriages. By 1969 it was estimated that more than half of unmarried college coeds were on oral contraceptives.
>
> The Pill sparked the sexual revolution. By separating sex from procreation, women were finally free to pursue pleasure without risk. And pursue it they did.[95]

## The National Organization for Women

While women were becoming more liberated in their personal lives, they continued to face discrimination in employment, education, and other areas. When Friedan observed the accomplishments of black civil rights organizations such as the National Association for the Advancement of Colored People (NAACP), she decided to form a similar organization to advance the rights of women. In 1966 Friedan and twenty-eight other women each contributed $5 as a seed fund for the National Organization for Women (NOW). With a start-up budget of $140, the group quickly raised more money, and before the year was out had set up seven task forces to study women's issues: family life, education, employment, media, religion, women in poverty, and women's legal and political rights.

By 1967 NOW was formally incorporated, with offices in Washington, D.C. Thanks to NOW lobbying, President Johnson signed a bill that prohibited sex discrimination in employment by the federal government and by contractors doing business with the government. After this victory, NOW focused on urging Congress to adopt the Equal Rights Amendment (ERA) to the Constitution. The amendment, which had first been proposed in 1923, read: "Equality of rights under the law shall not be denied or abridged by the United States or any state on account of sex."[96] Although this amendment sounded simple, attempts at passage touched off a political firestorm. Corporations claimed bankruptcy would result if women were paid as much as men. Military planners were afraid the ERA would force them to use women in combat roles. Some even argued that the amendment would force women and men to use the same public restrooms. NOW fought for passage of the ERA for years, but the amendment finally died in 1982.

NOW's political lobbying, however, did help women make some notable gains. In 1968 the Equal Employment Opportunity Commission ruled that employers could not place separate male and female "Help Wanted" ads in newspapers, and New York City newspapers such as the *New York Times, Post, Daily News* and *Village Voice* integrated their want ads.

Women made political advances as well. In 1968 NOW member Shirley Chisholm became the first African American women elected to the House of Representatives. This was a small

*In 1968, Shirley Chisholm became the first African American woman elected to the U.S. House of Representatives.*

victory—in 1969 out of 535 people serving in Congress there were only eleven women, although women made up 53.3 percent of the population of the United States.

In 1969 another NOW-backed victory for women was announced when the Fifth U.S. Court of Appeals ruled that women could not be barred from certain jobs because of lifting requirements. In this case, women were barred from working for the phone company at a position known as switchman because it was claimed that females could not lift thirty pounds. When this was proven false, women were hired for the higher-paying job. This ruling helped break down barriers for women in many industries where physical labor was required.

Meanwhile NOW generated continuing controversy with their support for abortion rights. At that time, terminating pregnancy by abortion was illegal in several states. NOW's pro-abortion position was vehemently opposed by the Catholic Church and several political organizations. Because of NOW's efforts in legal battles throughout the sixties, the Supreme Court legalized abortion in 1973.

## The Banner of Women's Liberation

While NOW fought battles for women's legal rights, tens of thousands of women in the United States were involved in "the Movement" that encompassed everything from student revolts to antiwar protests to Black, Chicano, and Native American power. While women were

*Women used tactics similar to those of counterculture protesters to bring attention to sexism and other causes.*

fighting for peace and equality for others, however, they discovered that the rights of women were ignored by the men who ran the protest organizations. The Sterns write: "When women stood up to demand that the issue of the sexism be addressed—at a meeting of the SDS or the Black Panthers—they were hooted down. Among hippies, Yippies, and Diggers, and on every tribal commune, women were *chicks*, which meant their job was to do womanly things such as bake [and] clean. . . ."[97]

While some women joined mainstream organizations such as NOW, more radical feminists, using protest tactics of the Yippies, garnered widespread media attention. Two weeks after the August 1968 Democratic Convention, a group of about two hundred women from an organization called New York Radical Women protested in front of the Miss America Pageant in Atlantic City, New Jersey. The Radical Women brought a sheep to the pageant to symbolize the mindless and docile image of

women that beauty contests represented. A flier handed out by the organization is reprinted in *The Times Were a Changin'*:

We will protest the image of Miss America, an image that oppresses women in every area in which it purports to represent us. There will be: Picket Lines; Guerrilla Theater; Leafleting; Lobbying Visits to the contestants urging our sisters to reject the Pageant Farce and join us; a huge Freedom Trash Can (into which we will throw bras, girdles, curlers, false eyelashes, wigs, and representative issues of *Cosmopolitan, Ladies' Home Journal, Family Circle*, etc.— bring any such woman-garbage you have around the house); we will also announce a Boycott of all those commercial products related to the Pageant, and the day will end with a Women's Liberation rally at midnight when Miss America is crowned on live television. Lots of other surprises are being

# The Women's Bill of Rights

The National Organization for Women ratified a Women's Bill of Rights in November 1967 that addressed many problems faced by average American women. It is reprinted in *The Times Were a Changin'*, edited by Irwin and Debi Unger.

"WE DEMAND:

I. That the U.S. Congress immediately pass the Equal Rights Amendment to the Constitution to provide that 'Equality of rights under the law shall not be denied or abridged by the United States or by any state on account of sex'. . . .

II. That equal employment opportunity be guaranteed to all women. . . .

III. That women be protected by law to ensure their rights to return to their jobs within a reasonable time after childbirth without loss of seniority . . . and be paid maternity leave. . . .

IV. Immediate revision of tax laws to permit the deduction of home and child-care expenses for working parents.

V. That child-care facilities be established by law on the same basis as parks, libraries, and public schools, adequate to the needs of children. . . .

VI. That the right of women to be educated to their full potential equally with men be secured by federal and state legislation, eliminating all discrimination and segregation by sex . . . at all levels of education, including colleges, graduate and professional schools, loans and fellowships, and federal and state training programs such as the Job Corps.

VII. The right of women in poverty to secure job training, housing, and family allowances on equal terms with men. . . . [and] revision of welfare legislation and poverty programs which deny women dignity, privacy, and self-respect.

VIII. The right of women to control their own reproductive lives by removing from the penal code laws limiting access to contraceptive information and devices, and by repealing penal laws governing abortion."

*Women attend a rally in New York City to promote the Equal Rights Amendment.*

planned (come and add your own!) but we do not plan heavy disruptive tactics and so do not expect a bad police scene. It should be a groovy day on the Boardwalk in the sun with our sisters. In case of arrests, however, we plan to reject all male authority and demand to be busted by policewomen only. (In Atlantic City, women cops are not permitted to make arrests—dig that!)

Male chauvinist-reactionaries on this issue had best stay away, nor are male liberals welcome in the demonstrations. But sympathetic men can donate money as well as cars and drivers.

Male reporters will be refused interviews. We reject patronizing reportage. *Only newswomen will be recognized*.[98]

One of the "special surprises" promised in the brochure came when protesters set off stink bombs inside the pageant hall. While authorities were attending to this diversion, protesters began chanting, "Freedom for women" and "No more Miss America."[99]

The demonstrators also held up a huge banner that read WOMEN'S LIBERATION. Camera operators inside the pageant focused on the banner, and this statement suddenly flashed across television sets throughout the world. It was the first time this mysterious phrase had ever been seen by the public at large, and few knew what it meant until it was explained in newspapers the next day. The protest by the New York Radical Women garnered more attention than the Miss America Pageant, and this demonstration became the first in a long series of media-grabbing events that were staged by women at the end of the sixties.

The "Freedom Trash Can" introduced by protesters that day soon became a regular icon at women's protest rallies. Women deposited their makeup, false eyelashes, dish towels, copies of *Playboy* and *Cosmopolitan*, and a few padded bras. These symbols were perceived as forcing women to live in stereotypical roles assigned by society.

## Burning Bras and Media Myths

Major media outlets soon began to mock and trivialize the women's movement, as it had done with the counterculture. *Time* called women's organizations "covens"—a term used to describe groups of witches. *Life* ran an article about a "girl in Chicago who described the progression of giving up short skirts, then makeup, and recently shaving her legs. 'I still look at my legs and think, oh my God, I cannot go through with this. I'll die for the revolution, but don't ask me not to shave my legs.'"[100]

Although women did not burn any undergarments at the September 7 Miss American Pageant, a journalist falsely reported that a burning bra was thrown in the Freedom Trash Can. Several weeks later a Chicago disc jockey paid three attractive fashion models to throw a few burning bras into a trashcan. This staged event was filmed, and the footage was shown repeatedly across the country. Since that time, the concept of "bra-burning feminists" became an entrenched myth in American culture.

Many women did stop wearing bras at that time. And according to the Sterns, this marked the end of "perky girl" sixties fashions:

Go-go boots, body stockings, outrageous make up, and tight jeans—formerly the fashion statements of free-thinking . . . chicks—became the symbolic shackles of male oppression. Liberated women abandoned flashy mod color schemes for the sake of Mother Nature earth tones. Baggy clothes and serious shoes or militaristic boots be-

*Lesbians and homosexuals demand equality under the law during a 1967 rally in Philadelphia.*

came a look of a proper woman revolutionary. For most militant feminists, hip-hugging miniskirts, gave way to shapeless unisex attire. . . . Among the militants, what you did with your hair became a sign of just how serious you were about the movement. . . . [It] was argued . . . that long hair meant you were living your life to please men—which was treason to the cause. . . . Conversely, hair under the arms and on legs had to stay.[101]

## Lesbian Rights

Although it was downplayed by groups such as NOW, many lesbians were involved in the feminist movement. In the era before gay rights, men and women who were homosexuals were virtually invisible to the large majority of the

American public. By the end of the 1960s, however, with almost every minority demanding equality, the gay and lesbian rights movement began to gain strength, as Farber explaines:

> For a committed radical feminist, dedicated to fighting women's dependence on men, at its root, lesbianism made a certain amount of ideological sense. In addition, the women's liberation movement really did attract the support of many lesbians, who without husbands to rely on for economic support, had more reason than most straight women to actively pursue gender equality.[102]

At that time there was extreme prejudice against lesbians and homosexuals in America, and many in the women's movement did not want to fight for gay rights while fighting for equality for the majority of nongay women.

*Members of NOW picket outside the White House in May of 1969 to promote the passage of the Equal Rights Amendment.*

The gay rights movement, however, took on a life of its own on June 27, 1969, when police raided the Stonewall Inn, a gay bar in Greenwich Village, New York. Although police had been raiding gay bars for years, this time the crowd began throwing beer cans and bottles at the police. Someone lit a fire in the bar, and the Stonewall Riot made headlines across the country. Within days lesbians joined homosexual men in spray painting the words GAY POWER on walls all over Greenwich Village. The Stonewall Riot marked the beginning of the gay liberation movement, which in the coming decades not only attempted to end social discrimination against lesbians and gay men, but also to promote pride among homosexuals.

## Feminism Becomes Mainstream

While gay rights and radical feminism remained controversial and alienated many Americans, the basic ideas behind the women's movement were difficult for anyone to refute—discrimination was wrong whether it was based on a person's religion, race, or gender. That some women reacted to it more angrily than others was a sign of the times during an angry decade that saw wars, riots, assassinations, and revolution in the streets. By 1970 NOW had more than 300,000 members with chapters in every state. Dozens of bestselling books and hundreds of magazine articles had exposed feminist theory to almost everyone in the United States.

In cities and suburbs across the country, women formed "consciousness-raising groups," where they could meet and discuss the personal details of their lives. At these sessions women often discovered that they had much in common. For the first time, women were able to openly discuss personal tragedies such as physical and sexual abuse or rape. As these problems were brought out into the open, support and counseling groups were formed and women were able to seek help where none had ever been available before.

As the ideas behind the feminist movement gained national prominence, terms such as "sexist" and "male chauvinist" joined the American lexicon with other sixties sayings such as "Do your own thing," and "Make love not war." And just as other sixties phenomenon had done, the voices of women joining together for equal rights had a profound and lasting impact on American culture—one that would permanently change life in the United States.

# Notes

## Introduction: A Nation Divided

1. Jane Stern and Michael Stern, *Sixties People*. New York: Alfred A. Knopf, 1990, p. 201.

## Chapter 1: Mainstream America

2. Myron A. Marty, *Daily Life in the United States: 1960–1990*. Westport, CT: Greenwood Press, 1997, p. 3.
3. David Farber, *The Great Age of Dreams: America in the 1960s*. New York: Hill and Wang, 1994, p. 10.
4. Stern and Stern, *Sixties People*, p. 201.
5. Farber, *The Great Age of Dreams*, p. 8.
6. Farber, *The Great Age of Dreams*, p. 22.
7. Marty, *Daily Life in the United States*, p. 8.
8. Farber, *The Great Age of Dreams*, p. 57.
9. John Javin and Gordon Javan, *60s!* New York: St. Martin's Press, 1983, p. 11.
10. Javin and Javan, *60s!*, pp. 46–47.
11. Farber, *The Great Age of Dreams*, pp. 53–54.
12. Tom Hayden, *Reunion: A Memoir*. New York: Random House, 1988, p. 114.
13. Quoted in Javin and Javan, *60s!*, p. 82.
14. Hayden, *Reunion*, pp. 113–14.
15. Farber, *The Great Age of Dreams*, p. 160.

## Chapter 2: African Americans in the Sixties

16. Farber, *The Great Age of Dreams*, p. 11.
17. Farber, *The Great Age of Dreams*, p. 77.
18. Quoted in Joan Morrison and Robert K. Morrison, eds., *From Camelot to Kent State: The Sixties Experience in the Words of Those Who Lived It*. New York: Times Books, 1987, p. 26.
19. Quoted in Morrison and Morrison, *From Camelot to Kent Stat*, p. 27.
20. Quoted in Henry Hampton and Steve Fayer, *Voices of Freedom*. New York: Bantam Books, 1990, p. 169.
21. Quoted in Lynda Rosen Obst, ed., *The Sixties*. New York: Rolling Stone Press, 1977, p. 156.
22. Quoted in Farber, *The Great Age of Dreams*, p. 114.
23. Quoted in Farber, *The Great Age of Dreams*, p. 115.
24. Farber, *The Great Age of Dreams*, p. 68.
25. Quoted in Time-Life Books, eds., *Turbulent Years: The 60s*. Alexandria, VA: Time-Life Books, 1998, p. 46.
26. Quoted in Farber, *The Great Age of Dreams*, p. 201.
27. Quoted in Peter B. Levy, *America in the Sixties Right, Left, and Center*. Westport, CT: Praeger, 1998, pp. 92, 95.
28. Sundiata Acoli, "A Brief History of the Black Panther Party and Its Place in the Black Liberation Movement," www.cs.oberlin.edu/students/pjaques/etext/acoli-hist-bpp.html, April 2, 1985.
29. Hampton and Fayer, *Voices of Freedom*, p. 350.
30. Quoted in Philip S. Foner, ed., *The Black Panthers Speak*. New York: Da Capo Press, 1995, pp. 5–6.
31. Stern and Stern, *Sixties People*. p. 191.
32. Quoted in Foner, *The Black Panthers Speak*, p. 263.
33. Quoted in Time-Life Books, *Turbulent Year*, p. 152.
34. Gillian G. Gaar, *She's a Rebel*. Seattle: Seal Press, 1992, pp. 86–87.

## Chapter 3: Counterculture

35. Quoted in Jack Kerouac, *On the Road*. New York: Signet, 1957, back cover.
36. Martin A. Lee and Bruce Shlain, *Acid Dreams*. New York: Grove Weidenfeld, 1992, p. 61.
37. Quoted in Barney Hoskyns, *Beneath the Diamond Sky: Haight-Ashbury 1965–1970*. New York: Simon & Schuster, 1997, p. 27.
38. Quoted in Lee and Shlain, *Acid Dreams*, p. 119.
39. Hoskyns, *Beneath the Diamond Sky*, pp. 33, 35.
40. Timothy Leary, *The Politics of Ecstasy*. Berkeley, CA: Ronin Publishing, 1998, p. 118.
41. Quoted in Farber, *The Great Age of Dreams*, p. 180.
42. Lee and Shlain, *Acid Dreams*, p. 141.
43. Farber, *The Great Age of Dreams*, p. 182.
44. Farber, *The Great Age of Dream*, p. 186.
45. Jerry Rubin, *Do It!* New York: Ballantine Books, 1970, pp. 55–56.
46. Emmett Grogan, *Ringolevio: A Life Played for Keeps*. New York: Citadel Underground Books, 1990, p. 247.
47. The Psychedelic 60s Home Page, www.lib.virginia.edu/exhibits/sixties/, August 17, 1999.
48. Stern and Stern, *Sixties People*, p. 163.
49. Stern and Stern, *Sixties People*, pp. 164, 166.
50. Timothy Miller, *The 60s Communes*. Syracuse, NY: Syracuse University Press, 1999, p. 15.
51. Miller, *The 60s Communes*, p. 39.
52. Quoted in Miller, *The 60s Communes*, p. 242.

## Chapter 4: The Soldiers

53. Quoted in Farber, *The Great Age of Dreams*, pp. 147–148.
54. Quoted in Richard Stacewicz, *Winter Soldiers: An Oral History of Vietnam Veterans Against the War*. New York: Twayne Publishers, 1997, p. 30.
55. Quoted in Stacewicz, *Winter Soldiers*, pp. 30–31.
56. Quoted in Stacewicz, *Winter Soldiers*, pp. 164–65.
57. Quoted in Stacewicz, *Winter Soldiers*, p. 184.
58. Alfred S. Bradford, *Some Even Volunteered*. Westport, CT: Praeger, 1994, pp. 3–4.
59. Quoted in Stacewicz, *Winter Soldiers*, p. 177.
60. Quoted in Stacewicz, *Winter Soldiers*, p. 41.
61. Quoted in Stacewicz, *Winter Soldiers*, p. 42.
62. Farber, *The Great Age of Dreams*, p. 151.
63. Farber, *The Great Age of Dreams*, p. 151.
64. Quoted in Stacewicz, *Winter Soldiers*, p. 148.
65. Quoted in Bob Greene, *Homecoming*. New York: G. P. Putnam's Sons, 1989, p. 24.
66. Quoted in Greene, *Homecoming*, pp. 128–29.
67. Quoted in Stacewicz, *Winter Soldiers*, p. 215.
68. Stacewicz, *Winter Soldiers*, p. 193.
69. Quoted in Stacewicz, *Winter Soldiers*, pp. 217–18.
70. Stacewicz, *Winter Soldiers*, p. 432.

## Chapter 5: The Protesters

71. Quoted in David Lance Goines, *The Free Speech Movement: Coming of Age in the 1960s*. Berkeley, CA: Ten Speed Press, 1993, pp. 365–66.
72. Rubin, *Do It!*, p. 24.
73. Rubin, *Do It!*, p. 38.
74. Nancy Zaroulis and Gerald Sullivan, *Who Spoke Up? American Protest Against the*

*War in Vietnam 1963–1975*, Garden City, NJ: Doubleday, 1984, p. 111.

75. Quoted in Jesse Kornbluth, *Notes from the New Underground*. New York: Viking Press, 1968, pp. 287–88.

76. Quoted in Clark Dougan and Samuel Lipsman eds., *A Nation Divided*. Boston: Boston Publishing, 1984, p. 73.

77. Terry H. Anderson, *The Movement and the Sixties*, New York: Oxford University Press, 1995, p. 145.

78. David Harris, *Our War: What We Did in Vietnam and What It Did to Us*. New York: Times Books, 1996, pp. 26–27.

79. Quoted in Morrison and Morrison, *From Camelot to Kent State*, p. 101.

80. Farber, *The Great Age of Dreams*, p. 149.

81. Dougan and Lipsman, *A Nation Divided*, pp. 77–78.

82. Farber, *The Great Age of Dreams*, p. 220.

83. Quoted in Morrison and Morrison, *From Camelot to Kent State*, pp. 271–72.

84. Quoted in Morrison and Morrison, *From Camelot to Kent State*, p. 273.

85. Charles Kaiser, *1968 in America*, New York: Weidenfield & Nicholson, 1988, pp. 162–63.

86. Abbie Hoffman, *Soon to Be a Major Motion Picture*. New York: Perigee Books, 1980, pp. 144–45.

87. Anderson, *The Movement and the Sixties*, pp. 223–24.

## Chapter 6: The Changing Roles of Women

88. June Sochen, *Herstory*. New York: Alfred Publishing, 1974, p. 382.

89. David Farber, *The Great Age of Dreams*, p. 241.

90. Sochen, *Herstory*, p. 390.

91. Quoted in Stern and Stern, *Sixties People*, pp. 19–20.

92. Stern and Stern, *Sixties People*, p. 19.

93. Quoted in Stern and Stern, *Sixties People*, p. 22.

94. Farber, *The Great Age of Dreams*, p. 250.

95. James R. Peterson, *The Century of Sex*. New York: Grove Press, 1999, p. 276.

96. Quoted in Unger and Unger, *The Times Were a Changin'*, p. 203.

97. Stern and Stern, *Sixties People*, p. 179.

98. Quoted in Unger and Unger, *The Times Were a Changin'*, p. 213.

99. Quoted in Farber, *The Great Age of Dreams*, p. 253.

100. Quoted in Stern and Stern, *Sixties People*, pp. 181–82.

101. Stern and Stern, *Sixties People*, p. 181.

102. Farber, *The Great Age of Dreams*, p. 258.

# For Further Reading

## Books

Barney Hoskyns, *Beneath the Diamond Sky: Haight-Ashbury 1965–1970*. New York: Simon & Schuster, 1997. A book with dozens of photographs and rainbow-colored pages that describe the social, cultural, political, and musical scene in America's premier hippie neighborhood during the late sixties. The author is an Oxford graduate who has written several books about music and films, including *Waiting for the Sun: Strange Days, Weird Scenes* and *Sound of Los Angeles*.

John Javin and Gordon Javan, *60s!* New York: St. Martin's Press, 1983. A book about the popular culture of the sixties illustrated with hundreds of photos of cars, fashions, comics, toys, movie posters, album covers, baseball cards, televisions stills, and more.

Lynda Rosen Obst, ed., *The Sixties*. New York: Rolling Stone Press, 1977. A book about the 1960s in the words of some famous people who lived through the decade. A year-by-year summary of famous events is recalled by Yippie Abbie Hoffman, Who band member Peter Townshend, civil rights leader Andrew Young, and others.

The oversize book is interspersed with full-page black-and-white photos of famous events both happy and tragic.

Jane Stern and Michael Stern, *Sixties People*. New York: Alfred A. Knopf, 1990. An entertaining book with chapters describing the music, fashion, and culture of surfers, folk singers, hippies, rebels, "Mr. and Mrs. Average," and other characters of the sixties along with many pages of photos, album art, and so on.

Time-Life Books, eds., *Turbulent Years: The 60s*. Alexandria, VA: Time-Life Books, 1998. A big colorful volume that covers all aspects of 1960s culture including the war in Vietnam, assassinations, hippies, communes, rock and roll, and the antiwar movement.

## Internet Sources

Daniel Walker, "Rights in Conflict," Chicago 1968 Democratic National Convention: Bibliography, www.geocities.com/Athens/Delphi/1553/ricsumm.html, 1999. A website maintained by Dean Blobaum that explores dozens of issues relating to the protests and violence at the 1968 Democratic Convention in Chicago.

# Works Consulted

## Books

Terry H. Anderson, *The Movement and the Sixties*. New York: Oxford University Press, 1995. A book that details the historic social movements of the 1960s from civil rights sit-ins to the antiwar marches to the women's liberation movement. The book explores the struggle for equality for African Americans, Native Americans, Chicanos, women, and others.

Alfred S. Bradford, *Some Even Volunteered*. Westport, CT: Praeger, 1994. The author, a history professor, faced heavy combat in Vietnam while serving in the First Wolfhounds, the nickname for the 127th Infantry from Fort Benning, Georgia. His narrative of Vietnam is extremely informative, compelling, and sometimes bitingly humorous. After watching his friends die and studying the war and his role in it, the author explains why the United States lost the war.

Clark Dougan and Samuel Lipsman, eds., *A Nation Divided*. Boston: Boston Publishing, 1984. One of the books in the Vietnam Experience series. This edition explores events in the United States during the Vietnam War including the protest movement, the pro-war movement, and media coverage of the events.

David Farber, *The Great Age of Dreams: America in the 1960s*. New York: Hill and Wang, 1994. A history of the 1960s written from the perspective of the commonly held vision of the American dream and how the Vietnam War, rise of the counterculture, big-city riots, and other sixties conflicts disrupted that dream.

Philip S. Foner, ed., *The Black Panthers Speak*. New York: Da Capo Press, 1995. A book of writings by Black Panther founders Bobby Seale, Huey Newton, and others. The book highlights positive Panther programs such as free lunches and medical clinics in black neighborhoods, along with the party's record of police confrontations, court battles, and other information.

Betty Friedan, *The Feminine Mystique*. New York: Norton, 1963. The groundbreaking book about the lives of suburban women in the early sixties and the unhappiness faced by many because of gender discrimination.

Gillian G. Gaar, *She's a Rebel*. Seattle: Seal Press, 1992. A well-researched book about the contribution women have made to rock and roll history from the 1940s to the 1990s.

David Lance Goines, *The Free Speech Movement: Coming of Age in the 1960s*. Berkeley, CA: Ten Speed Press, 1993. A book that studies the social and cultural aspects of the Berkeley Free Speech Movement, which quickly transformed into the antiwar movement.

Bob Greene, *Homecoming*. New York: G. P. Putnam's Sons, 1989. The author, a syndicated columnist, asked Vietnam veterans about their experiences when they returned home, specifically if they were ever spat upon by American citizens.

Emmett Grogan, *Ringolevio: A Life Played for Keeps*. New York: Citadel Underground Books, 1990. The autobiography of the founder of the Diggers, San Francisco's urban guerrillas who provided free food to the thousands of runaway teens who descended on the city during the late sixties.

Henry Hampton and Steve Fayer, *Voices of Freedom*. New York: Bantam Books, 1990. An oral history of the civil rights movement from the 1950s through the 1980s, in the words of those who witnessed and participated in famous events. A literary companion to the public television series *Eyes on the Prize*, this volume gives life to the exciting—and often tragic—battles waged by African Americans in order to gain equality in the United States.

David Harris, *Our War: What We Did in Vietnam and What It Did to Us*. New York: Times Books, 1996. Harris, married to folk singer Joan Baez, was one of the more famous draft resisters of the sixties. In the movie *Woodstock,* Baez dedicates a song to Harris, who at the time was serving two years in a federal prison for refusing admission into the army.

Tom Hayden, *Reunion: A Memoir*. New York: Random House, 1988. An autobiography by a man who was one of the founding members of the SDS, led dozens of protests in the sixties, and was put on trial for conspiracy after the Chicago Democratic Convention. Hayden later went on to marry actress Jane Fonda and served many years as a state assemblyman in California.

Abbie Hoffman, *Soon to Be a Major Motion Picture*. New York: Perigee Books, 1980. An autobiography of Abbie Hoffman that details his childhood in Massachusetts and his elevation to a national leader and founder of the Yippies.

Peter Joseph, ed., *Good Times: An Oral History of America in the Nineteen Sixties*. New York: Charterhouse, 1973. The history of the sixties as told by people who witnessed the rallies, riots, and countercultural events.

Charles Kaiser, *1968 in America*. New York: Weidenfeld & Nicholson, 1988. Nineteen sixty-eight was the most chaotic year of the sixties and one of the most turbulent in American history. This book covers the music, politics, commotion, counterculture, and experimentation that shaped a generation.

Jesse Kornbluth, *Notes from the New Underground*. New York: Viking Press, 1968. A book written in the sixties with essays from the underground press regarding the counterculture, American culture, the Vietnam War, and radical politics.

Timothy Leary, *The Politics of Ecstasy*. Berkeley, CA: Ronin Publishing, 1998. A provocative book written by a man who advocated widespread use of LSD by the general population. The former Harvard psychology professor enunciates his views on the social and political ramifications of psychedelic drug use.

Martin A. Lee and Bruce Shlain, *Acid Dreams*. New York: Grove Weidenfeld, 1992. A book that explores the social history of LSD from the CIA's 1950s obsession with it as a secret weapon to the widespread use of the drug during the hippie era of the 1960s. The authors unearthed twenty thousand documents from secret government files in order to paint a startling picture of the CIA's involvement in one of the largest drug experiments in history.

Peter B. Levy, *America in the Sixties Right, Left, and Center*. Westport, CT: Praeger, 1998. This book tells the history of the sixties in documents, articles, and journalism from that era, including Johnson's Great Society speech, Martin Luther King's "Letter from a Birmingham City Jail," and other historic words.

Myron A. Marty, *Daily Life in the United States: 1960–1990*, Westport, CT: Greenwood Press, 1997. A history book that explores the lives of average Americans from the space age to the computer age.

Timothy Miller, *The 60s Communes*. Syracuse, NY: Syracuse University Press, 1999. A volume that details the widespread move toward communal living between the early 1960s and mid-1970s.

Joan Morrison and Robert K. Morrison, eds., *From Camelot to Kent State: The Sixties*

*Experience in the Words of Those Who Lived It*. New York: Times Books, 1987. The personal stories of fifty-nine men and women who lived through the 1960s. In their own words, they recall the civil rights movement, assassinations, protesting the Vietnam War, and joining the counterculture revolution.

James R. Peterson, *The Century of Sex*. New York: Grove Press, 1999. A history of the sexual revolution.

Jerry Rubin, *Do It!* New York: Ballantine Books, 1970. One of the most radical books of the sixties, written by the founder of the Yippies. He tells students to drop out, resist authority, and foment revolution against schools, government, corporations, and society. *Do It!* traces Rubin's life from a straitlaced sports reporter to a revolutionary agitator against the Vietnam War in the late sixties.

June Sochen, *Herstory*. New York: Alfred Publishing, 1974. The author, a professor of history at Northwestern University, presents the women's side of American history and details the life stories and experiences of an often-ignored group of people who helped make the United States one of the most successful countries in the world.

Richard Stacewicz, *Winter Soldiers: An Oral History of Vietnam Veterans Against the War*. New York: Twayne Publishers, 1997. The author brings together more than thirty former Vietnam veterans and members of the Vietnam Veterans Against the War. The book poignantly records the words of the vets as they discuss Vietnam and their experiences after they were discharged and became leaders in the antiwar movement.

Irwin Unger and Debi Unger, eds., *The Times Were a Changin'*. New York: Three Rivers Press, 1998. An anthology of "speeches, manifestos, court decisions, and groundbreaking journalism" of the sixties, with excerpts from documents concerning the antiwar movement, women's liberation, the race to the moon, and other compelling subjects.

Nancy Zaroulis and Gerald Sullivan, *Who Spoke Up? American Protest Against the War in Vietnam 1963–1975*. Garden City, NY: Doubleday, 1984. A year-by-year record of the actions of those who spoke out against the Vietnam War along with the triumphs and failures of the antiwar movement.

## Internet Sources

Sundiata Acoli, "A Brief History of the Black Panther Party and Its Place in the Black Liberation Movement," www.cs.oberlin.edu/students/pjaques/etext/acoli-hist-bpp.html, April 2, 1985. A website with a paper written by an imprisoned Black Panther detailing the history of the Black Panther Party.

The Diggers Archives Home Page, www.diggers.org/. In their own words: "The Digger Archives is an ongoing Web project to preserve and present the history of the anarchist guerilla street theater group that challenged the emerging Counterculture of the Sixties and whose actions and ideals inspired (and continue to inspire) a generation (of all ages)."

The Psychedelic 60s Home Page, www.lib.virginia.edu/exhibits/sixties/, August 17, 1999. A website run by the University of Virginia Library Special Collections Department with colorful and informative facts about the 1960s counterculture including information about the music, artwork, fashion, and protest.

Steven C. Teel, Storytellers, www.kn.pacbell.com/wired/fil/pages/listushisst1.html An Internet resource on U.S. history that contains over a hundred links to websites that feature oral histories of the Vietnam War, the antiwar protests, the Free Speech Movement, the psychedelic sixties, women's history, the civil rights movement, and dozens of other events remembered firsthand by those who lived through them.

# Index

# Picture Credits

# About the Author

Stuart A. Kallen is the author of over more than 150 nonfiction books for children and young adults. He has written on topics ranging from the theory of relativity to rock-and-roll history to life on the American frontier. In addition, Mr. Kallen has written award-winning children's videos and television scripts. In his spare time, Stuart A. Kallen is a singer/songwriter/guitarist in San Diego, California.